Bum Fodder

Bum Fodder

An Absorbing
History of Toilet Paper

RICHARD SMYTH

Souvenir Press

1. Beginnings

Bumfodder, n. Also *bumf, bumph*. Toilet paper.

Oxford English Dictionary

To wipe is human.

And for most of us in the western world, to wipe is to wipe with paper. In the UK alone, the market is worth around £600 million a year; worldwide, toilet paper equivalent to some 27,000 trees is flushed away every single day. In the US, in particular, loo-roll use has assumed gargantuan proportions; the average American uses 57 sheets per day, or 20,805 sheets per year – 50 per cent more than the average Brit. In total, Americans spend $8 billion a year on toilet paper.

But for all our Andrex and our Charmin, our multi-ply and our super-soft, we are only ever playing catch-up in this field of endeavour. We are always riding – or, rather, wiping – on someone else's coat-tails.

As with all great inventions, China got there first.

They got there first with the decimal system, the compass, the wheelbarrow, silk, printing and gunpowder, and it's probably only a matter of time before archaeo-sinologists dig up a Han dynasty SmartPhone – and they got there first with toilet-paper, too.

The first step was the invention of paper. They did that in around 100 CE: somewhat improbably, it's attributed to a single man, T'sai Lun, who derived sheets of proto-paper from a mash of mulberry, fishing nets, old rags, and hemp waste.

Sadly, the name of the first man to apply this cutting-edge technology to his backside has been lost to posterity. But we *do* know that paper had made the transition from craft material to bumfodder by the end of the 6th century. In 589, the refined scholar and court official Yan Zhitui agonised over the below-stairs deployment of fine literature:

> Paper on which there are quotations or commentaries from Five Classics or the names of sages, I dare not use for toilet purposes.

During the 9th century, a Muslim visitor to China remarked that the Chinese 'are not careful about cleanliness, and they do not wash themselves with water when they have done their necessities; but they only wipe themselves with paper'.

A few hundred years later, the Chinese toilet-paper industry was booming. In the early 14th century, during the reign of the Yuang dynasty, a million packets of toilet-paper, each comprising between a thousand and ten thousand sheets, were being produced each year in Zhejiang province alone – but then, there are a lot of people in China (the population of Zhejiang's major city, Lin'an, was around a million in 1275), and therefore, it can safely be assumed, a lot of bottoms.

In 1393, seven hundred and twenty thousand 2ft × 3ft sheets were manufactured for the sole use of the Imperial court at Nanjing; according to the Imperial Bureau of Supplies, a further fifteen thousand sheets were made for the family of the Emperor, Hongwu. These sheets were made particularly soft, to suit delicate royal behinds, and were perfumed. Such sensitivity was not typical of Hongwu: having started life as a starving orphan and progressed to the Imperial throne via a career as a wandering mendicant, he was, by any standard, a brutal despot. Among his many innovations was the use at court of heavy bamboo, as what we might today call a performance incentive for the civil service. Under Hongwu's rule, many a scholar-official was beaten to death with bamboo staves for the least infraction.

The story of the Emperor's toilet paper serves as a reminder that even vicious dictators have their tender spots.

In China, Burma and Vietnam, much toilet paper is still manufactured by hand; the International Paper Museum at the Research Institute of Paper History and Technology in Brookline, Massachussetts, claims to have the world's largest collection of this kind of paper.

But 2ft × 3ft mulberry-based toilet-paper sheets are not what we would normally expect to arrive in our supermarket delivery when we have ticked the box for 'Loo Rolls, SuperSaver Family Pack'. We have come a long way since Hongwu's day.

In fact, it might be said that millions of people in the world today exist in a post-paper age. They would certainly say so in Kokura, Japan – the ancestral home of the Washlet.

Just as the Chinese dragged bum-cleansing into the 6th century with their high-tech mulberry wipes, their neighbours across the East China Sea have applied third-millennium science to bringing the practice bang up to date.

Toyo Toki Ltd was founded in Kokura by Kazuchika Okura in 1917 to bring western-style 'sanitary ceramics' to a Japan in which wooden bathroom-ware was still the order of the day. Renamed Toto, the firm soon came to dominate the burgeoning Japanese sanitaryware market. Then, in 1980, Toto launched the Washlet. The future had arrived. We weren't in Kansas any more.

The product of many years' research in bottom-centric ergonomics, the Washlet delivered a triple-whammy of toilet comforts: its heated seat kept your buttocks cosy, a jet of warm water hosed you down, and a gust of air dried you off.

An iconic TV advert made the case for the new technology. A winsome young girl in a floral dress tries to wipe a dollop of black ink from her hand with a paper tissue – but succeeds only in making a dreadful mess. Oh no!

'Paper won't fully clean it,' the girl explains to camera. 'It's the same with your bottom.'

Cut to a forbidding-looking Washlet nozzle, which promptly squirts a jet of water four feet into the air. The proceedings are brought to a close by the girl presenting her bottom to the viewer and a jovial choir performing the 'Toto Washlet!' jingle.

Early indications were that Japan was not ready for the Washlet revolution. The TV advert triggered a flood of complaints from resolutely old-school Japanese toilet-goers. First this porcelain nonsense, the trend of conservative thought seems to have been, and now paper-free cleansing! Whatever next? They probably weren't much mollified by another ad that warned: 'Don't let people say behind your back that you have a dirty bottom!'

But the Luddites – as usual – lost out. By 2009, 72 per cent of Japanese households were equipped with a Washlet or equivalent device (bear in mind that, at the same time, only 30 per cent had a dishwasher). Having taken 18 years to sell its first 10 million Washlets, Toto announced in February 2011 that they had just sold their 30 millionth. The Petit Washlet, a fold-away model that could be carried in a lady's handbag, broke further new ground. The most up-to-date model – the Toto Neolet Washlet-integrated Toilet – features a remote control, a sensor-operated lid that opens and closes automatically, a 'tornado flush', an air filter, and a range of rinsing options (from 'soft wash' to – hold on tight! – 'oscillating wash').

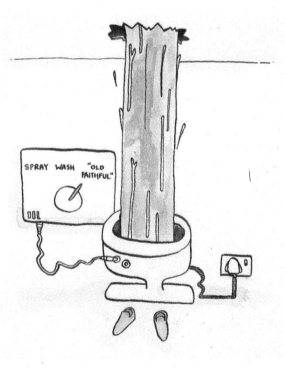

This is a brave new world indeed. How did we get here? Well, it's been a long journey. The road has not been easy; it has, on the contrary, been bumpy, uncomfortable, and at times startlingly abrasive.

It's a journey that, like all journeys, comes with a story. This is the story of mankind's pursuit of gentleness in an unforgiving world. It is the story, in short, of bumfodder.

2. Experiments

'A fool is a man who has never tried an experiment in his life.'

Erasmus Darwin

Hygiene in one form or another is a concept that's been observed throughout the animal kingdom. Birds keep their nests clean and tidy, ants groom themselves to remove fungal pathogens, even nematode worms steer clear of their disease-carrying peers – so, inevitably, we don't have the sharp end of this particularly pyramid entirely to ourselves.

To wipe might be human, but it doesn't separate us from the animals. They do it too.

The chimpanzees of central Africa are our principal co-wipers. Jane Goodall is one of a number of primate scientists to have observed mother chimps diligently wiping their children's behinds with leaves; adults (who have also been known to swab down their private parts after sex) often work the same trick on themselves, especially if faecal matter has got somewhere it shouldn't be. One study reported that an adult male 'wiped feces from his back soiled by another male using a leafy twig' – before, one imagines, having a quiet but firm word with the other male in question.

But we have managed to distance ourselves in this regard

from our hairier cousins (and, presumably, from our remote, pre-human ancestors); we – particularly in the western world – have made wiping a matter of primary importance to our personal hygiene. In the age of tri-ply quilted softness with aloe vera, a 'leafy twig' just won't cut it.

The reasons for this are – like many a sheet of toilet paper – twofold.

Firstly, our upright ambulation – that is, our quirky habit of walking on two legs instead of scrambling about on all fours – requires us to have large, muscular bottoms. Our buttocks may not glow red to attract members of the opposite sex, as those of some baboon species do, but they certainly have the edge in muscularity. These heavily bunched walking machines of ours, however, are something of an impediment to rear-end hygiene – particularly when the second key factor that has pushed bottom-wiping to the centre of our toilet routine is taken into consideration.

Our insistence on sitting upright while defecating bedevils the bottoms of the western world. From the seated (and communal) latrines of ancient Rome to the Elizabethan 'Ajax' or water-closet of John Harington (the spiritual father of the British loo), our lavatorial contrivances have served to distance us from the healthful practice of voiding our waste in the way nature intended: by adopting what we might call the Primordial Squat.

According to Dave Praeger, author of the fearfully comprehensive *Poop Culture*, it is only by squatting that we allow the folds of the rectal cavity (Praeger calls them 'baffles') to be fully opened; when we sit, these folds are open only half-way, which is why the whole business can sometimes be a bit of a struggle.

Praeger points to claims (widely made by practitioners of

alternative medicine, but that doesn't *necessarily* mean they're a lot of bunk) that cultures that eschew the seated toilet also have lower rates of haemorrhoids, appendicitis, irritable bowel syndrome, diverticulosis, colorectal cancer, bladder incontinence and prostate cancer.

What's *certainly* true is that, whatever's going on inside, those who squat, rather than sit, wind up with substantially less wiping to do. We in the west choose, as a rule, to sit – and, thus, to wipe.

So: bottom-wiping is a *principally* human activity.

It is also a singularly refined one, in the sense of 'refinement' as a gradual process of experiment and selection, a long-term winnowing in pursuit of the best possible solution to a fundamental problem.

This process is, of course, the coping-stone of the scientific method. Many great scientists have also been great experimenters: one thinks of Benjamin Franklin flying a kite on a copper wire during a lightning-storm, or Francis Bacon catching a fatal chill while attempting to refrigerate a chicken (and one concludes that, as well as great experimenters, many great scientists have also been idiots). Without bold experimentation, how would we know what happens when you transplant a cockerel's testicle into a chicken's gut? The answer – discovered by the 18th century surgeon John Hunter – is that the testicle does quite well (but that the cockerel nurses a lasting grievance). Hunter was also responsible for the finding that human semen, 'held some time in the mouth, produces a warmth similar to spices, which lasts some time'.

Britain – home to Hunter and Bacon, Newton and Faraday – was in many ways the cradle of the experimental method, the *fons et origo* of suck-it-and-see. But, in the contest to find the most fearless experimenter of them all, Britain must cede to France – to a Frenchman who (a) never existed and (b) was a giant.

Le Bumfourrage

Gargantua is the over-sized son of Grangousier and the father of Pantagruel in François Rabelais' 16th century masterpiece *Gargantua and Pantagruel.*

Rabelais was a priest and scholar from the province of Poitou in western France. He was renowned throughout his life as a deeply learned man – and, at the same time, mistrusted because of his attachment to jokes about toilets and genitals. The *Gargantua* books – which began with *The Horrible and Terrifying Deeds and Words of the Renowned Pantagruel, King of the Dipsodes* in 1532 – are a reckless swirl of parody, grotesquery and wordplay (Rabelais published them under the pseudonym Alcofribas Nasier, a none-too-cunning anagram of his real name). The lives of Gargantua and Pantagruel are explored in riotous and vivid detail, beginning with the birth of Gargantua out of his mother's left ear. His first act is to cry for drink; such is his size and gluttony, it takes seventeen thousand, nine hundred and thirteen cows to provide his milk – with inevitably messy consequences.

> He cried very little, but beshit himself every hour: for to speak truly of him, he was wonderfully phlegmatick in his posteriors, both by reason of his natural complexion and ... his much quaffing of the septembral juyce.

Learned commentators will tell you that *Gargantua and Pantagruel* is a learned satire of the *mores* of the fifteen-thirties, peppered with erudite swipes at the religio-aristocratic establishment and highbrow gags designed to raise a knowing titter among the French *intelligentsia* – and they will be correct. They will point out that Rabelais took pot-shots at avaricious lawyers because he had seen his own father chiselled in the pursuit of wasteful lawsuits, and satirised quack doctors because he himself was trying to make a living as an honest physician – and in this, too, they will probably be correct.

However, they will also tell you that those who relish Rabelais simply for his fanatical devotion to the lowest order of juvenile humour are somehow missing the point – and in this they will be quite wrong, for it could hardly be clearer that Rabelais himself rejoiced in all things puerile, outrageous and childishly hilarious, and there's nothing remotely wrong with joining in with the toilet-humour sniggers while skimming over the cutting remarks about contemporary heraldry.

The straightforward fact is that Rabelais, had he been so inclined, *could* have written a five-volume satire of Europe under the yoke of Holy Roman Emperor Charles V and not included *any* fart-gags, codpiece jokes or lists of synonyms for the male genitals. He didn't. Good for him.

Gargantua's great experiment – or, rather, programme of experiments – is one of the highlights of Book One. Old Grangousier, returning from the wars, asks his son, the massive and oft-pooping Gargantua, whether he has managed to keep himself 'sweet and clean'. Gargantua says that he certainly has – for he has, 'by a long and curious experience, found out a means to wipe my bum, the most lordly, the most excellent, and the most convenient that ever was seen'.

The giant's quest – his 'long and curious experience' – begins, perhaps surprisingly, in the ladies' accessories department:

> Once I did wipe me with a gentle-woman's velvet mask, and found it to be good; for the softness of the silk was very voluptuous and pleasant to my fundament. Another time with one of their hoods, and in like manner that was comfortable. At another time with a lady's neckerchief, and after that I wiped me with some ear-pieces of hers made of crimson satin, but there was such a number of golden spangles in them (turdy round things, a pox take them) that they fetched away all the skin of my tail with a vengeance.

Gargantua goes on to wish 'St Anthony's Fire' on the 'bumgut' of the goldsmith responsible for the spangles ('St Anthony's Fire' can refer to any one of three unpleasant diseases – ergotism, erysipelas, and shingles – none of which any goldsmith of sensitivity would want in or near his bumgut).

Changing tack, the giant prodigy, finding himself behind a bush, experiments with a 'March-cat' – but the results aren't encouraging. 'Her claws were so sharp,' Gargantua ruefully reports, 'that they scratched and exulcerated all my perinee.'

A wipe with his mother's gloves relieves the discomfort, and the experiments continue; a basketful of greengroceries provide the next batch of potential 'wipebreeches' (or *torcheculs*, in Gargantuan jargon).

Sage, fennel, anet (i.e. dill), marjoram, roses, beets, cole-wort (a kind of cabbage), vine-leaves, lettuce and spinach leaves are all tested and found wanting, as are parsley, nettles and comfrey. Never let a French giant near your organic veg box. The comfrey gives Gargantua 'the bloody flux of Lombardy', which, mysteriously, he cures by wiping himself with his own codpiece. And on we go, as the giant sets about the soft furnishings:

> Then I wiped my tail in the sheets, in the coverlet, in the curtains, with a cushion, with arras hangings, with a green carpet, with a table-cloth, with a napkin, with a handker-chief, with a combing-cloth ... I wiped myself with hay, with straw, with thatch-rushes, with flax, with wool, with paper ... with a kerchief, with a pillow, with a pantoufle, with a pouch, with a pannier.

Gargantua then tries out a number of different kinds of hats, concluding: 'The best of all these is the shaggy hat, for it makes a very neat abstersion of the fecal matter.'

The giant's inquiries lead him into ever-stranger territory, as first a barnyard ('with a hen, with a cock, with a pullet, with a calf's skin, with a hare, with a pigeon ...') and then an assortment of bric-a-brac ('with an attorney's bag, with a mon-tero [a kind of Spanish hunting cap], with a coif, with a falconer's lure ...') is brought to ruin.

Finally, Gargantua comes to the upshot. What, having con-cluded his exhaustive and eye-watering survey, does the giant conclude is 'the most lordly, the most excellent, and the most convenient' means of wiping his bum? What, 'of all torcheculs, arsewisps, bumfodders, tail-napkins, bunghole cleansers, and wipe-breeches', does Gargantua declare the finest?

REYNARD THE ASS-PIZZLE

One notable exception or escapee from Gargantua's list is the fox. But don't worry: the critter makes a memorable appearance elsewhere in Rabelais' masterpiece. Pantagruel, by way of illustrating the excellence of the fox's tail as an 'ass-pizzle', tells the following story, which is decidedly not for the faint hearted.

A lion, having been wounded with an axe, is told by a friendly carpenter that he must wipe the wound so 'that the flies might not do their excrements in it', and then fill it with moss. Thus healed, the lion proceeds on his way until he encounters an old woman, who falls over in fright – disclosing to the lion her naked underparts. What follows is probably what Rabelaisians would see as a hilarious misunderstanding. 'They have hurt this good woman here between the legs most villainously,' the lion concludes.

We won't go into the unseemly detail, save to say that a lush-brushed passing fox is summoned to help.

'God hath furnished thee with a tail,' the lion urges. 'Thou hast a long one, and of a bigness proportionable; wipe hard, and be not weary . . .'

The neck of a live goose. It seems so obvious when you think about it.

On submitting the unfortunate fowl to this indignity, Gargantua promises, 'you will thereby feel in your nockhole a most wonderful pleasure, both in regard of the softness of the said down and of the temperate heat of the goose, which is easily communicated to the bum-gut and the rest of the inwards, in so far as to come even to the regions of the heart and brains'.

Elizabethan courtier John Harington, the inventor of the water-closet and author of the jocular and epoch-making toilet treatise *The Metamorphosis of Ajax* (1596), was rather contemptuous of Rabelais (whom he supposed to be 'a clerk of the stole [stool] to some prince of the blood of France'). In *Ajax*, he dismissed Gargantua's programme of experiments as 'a beastly treatise' in which the writer alleges that:

white paper is too smooth, brown paper too rough, woollen cloth too stiff, linen cloth too hollow, satin too slippery, taffeta too thin, velvet too thick, or perhaps too costly . . .

Harington, who may have been having a joke himself, is probably responsible for the enduring misconception that Gargantua's quest was in fact Rabelais's, and that the entire revolting litany, goose and all, was meant to be taken seriously.

Indeed, some people have subsequently taken it so seriously as to link it, through the medium of the urban legend, with one of our most revered modern deities: Elvis Presley.

In a 2000 interview with the rock-music weekly NME, Liam Gallagher, the lead singer of the British band Oasis, was asked what the reason was for his 'fascination' with the King. Liam's reply, which left his interviewer briefly (and understandably) stumped, was: 'My fascination with Elvis? Just the wiping his arse with gooses' necks does it for me, man. That just kills me.'

Asked to elaborate, Liam explained: 'He'd have a big box of or bucket of gooses' necks that had just been chopped off . . . and he'd wipe his arse out the window with gooses' necks . . . He is the king. That's what kings do, innit? You know what I mean? They do, don't they?'

There is, however, no evidence that the King – or, indeed, any king – actually put Gargantua's advice into practice.

Today's top-end toilet-roll brands strive to offer as near an approximation as possible of the heavenly touch of warm goose-neck, and so it could be said that we have ourselves, at last, with our Pillowsoft, our Cushelle and our Nouvelle, our Triple Softy, our Gorgeous Comfort Quilts and our Touch Of Luxury, achieved Rabelais' toilet Nirvana. But, much like Gargantua, we had to go to some quite considerable lengths to get there.

3. The Wisdom Of The Ancients

'Who can bring a clean thing out of an unclean? Not one.'

the Book of Job, Chapter 14, Verse 3

One of the principal difficulties in compiling a history of the wipebreech is the fact that wipers since the dawn of human history have, through a combination of unreasoning contempt and unnecessary embarrassment, preferred not to dwell on the act of bum-wiping (despite engaging in the practice on at least a daily basis). Bumfodder is ephemeral; bumfodder is born to be flushed away. All too often – and not unironically – bum-fodder has left no mark upon the historical record.

No-one in Shakespeare, for instance, wipes their bottoms. There is no cry of 'Once more unto the wipebreech!' in *Henry V*; it is not an arsewisp that Macbeth sees before him, and the friends, Romans and countrymen are not asked to lend Mark Antony their bunghole-cleansers. Evidently even Shakespeare – 'the nearest thing incarnation to the eye of God', according to Sir Laurence Olivier – considered bum-fodder as being beneath his notice.

Even the one chronicler who we might think would have been willing to set down the details of his torcheculing for the enjoyment and improvement of posterity turns out to have shied away from the task. Samuel Pepys was a tireless recorder not only of the intrigues of 17th-century City business (and of his many adulterous rogueries) but also of his somewhat excruciating daily toilet habits.

At the end of his entry for May 19, 1664 – to take just one of many examples – Pepys reports: 'A pretty good stool, which I impute to my whey to-day, and broke wind also.' On another occasion, in 1665, he ran into difficulties while staying at new lodgings: 'Feeling for a chamber-pott, there was none . . . so I was forced in this strange house to rise and shit in the chimney twice; and so to bed and was very well again.'

You would imagine that a man who owns up so frankly to defecating in another man's chimney wouldn't scruple to inform his public of his post-evacuation procedures. But no: in all of Pepys' abundant memoir, bumfodder merits no mention at all.

The same goes for Captain John G Bourke's unreliable but eye-popping anthropological classic *Scatalogic Rites Of All Nations* (1891). A book that finds room for entire chapters on 'The Ordure Of The Grand Lama Of Tibet', 'Tolls Of Flatulence Exacted Of Prostitutes In France', 'The Onion Adored By The Egyptians' and 'The Use Of Bladders In Making Excrement Sausages' somehow manages to skirt the subject of wiping up afterwards, save one or two cursory mentions.

Things are similarly opaque when we seek to peer further back in time. Aristotle might famously have observed that 'all men by nature desire to know', but he shed no light on this most fascinating of subjects. The Roman Lucretius wrote lengthily *On The Nature Of Things*, but the nature of this particular thing was not, alas, within his compass.

So the obvious sources fail us. We have to dig deeper.

Beware Greeks Bearing Bumfodder

For the great Milanese archaeologist Guido Calza (1888–1946), the ancient port city of Ostia, on the west coast of Italy at the mouth of the river Tiber, was *non solo un campo di studio, ma un centro di vita per ogni sua facoltà* – not only a field of study, but a centre of life for every human faculty. Nothing among the many discoveries Calza unearthed at Ostia – from the *horrea* of Epagathus and Epaphroditus to the necropolis of the *Isola Sacra* – embodies this vision of the city as emphatically as does his find of 1936, the *Terme dei Sette Sapienti* – the Baths of the Seven Sages.

The Seven Sages were wise men of Greece, supposed to have lived around 600 BCE. Their names were Cleobulus of Lindos, Solon of Athens, Chilon of Sparta, Bias of Priene, Thales of Miletus, Pittacus of Mytilene, and Periander of Corinth.

In Greek tradition, the Sages each embodied a different aspect of wisdom. To each was attributed a pithy soundbite or catchphrase; 'Avoid excess', for instance, was one of Solon's, while Thales' snappy 'Know thyself' was later engraved on the façade of the Oracle of Apollo at Delphi.

However, by the second century CE, reverence for these semi-mythic sages appears to have been on the wane. The anonymous Roman painter who decorated the walls of the *Terme dei Sette Sapienti* evidently knew his Greek history: Solon, Thales, Chilon and Bias are all up there (and it's believed that Pittacus, Periander and Cleobulus once were, too). But these Sages aren't the maxim-happy moralists of time-honoured tradition.

Solon – lawmaker, poet and statesman – is graced by the surtitle 'To Shit Well, Solon Stroked His Belly'. To the sage classically venerated as the originator of the maxim 'You should not desire the impossible' is attributed a more earthy revelation: 'Cunning Chilon Taught How To Flatulate Unnoticed'. Thales, who in reality earned renown for his hypothesis of a cosmology based on water as the essence of all matter, is immortalised by the Ostia satirist as recommending only that 'Those Who Shit Hard Should Really Work At It'.

Depicted beneath the toilet-fixated Sages are a bunch of ordinary Roman men, seated, it seems, upon a communal latrine. The banter here is coming thick and fast: 'Push hard, you'll be finished more quickly', chides one – 'I'm hurrying,' his companion protests – a third, more obscurely, offers: 'You're sitting on a mule-driver!'

Another man chips in: 'No one gives you a long lecture, Priscianus, as long as you use the sponge on a stick . . .'

Ah, the sponge on a stick: the cherished *xylospongion*.

The sixteenth-century French essayist Michel de Montaigne, in an account of some of the habits of the ancient world, explained that the *spongion* – 'the reason why 'Spongia' in Latin is counted an obscene word' – was always tied to the end of a 'gaffe' or rod (Montaigne also tells us that, 'having ended the delights of nature [i.e. sex], they were wont to wipe their privities with perfumed wool').

But, given a moment's thought, the very existence of the sponge on a stick raises questions. The foremost is surely, why a stick? A sponge, yes: a tidy and efficacious alternative to a fig leaf, a bare hand, or a fistful of moss. But why the foot-long stick?

In answering this question during a talk at a primary school, historian Caroline Lawrence was confronted by a pupil with an alarming suggestion: 'Please miss, is it to get it further up your bum?'

It is not – as far as we know – for that (the Romans were known for their thoroughness, but even they had their limits). In fact, it has to do with good old-fashioned modesty.

A Roman latrine had two holes in it. One, course, was on the top. That's what we might call the business entrance. The other was at the front, and was smaller: we can think of this as the service entrance. When a Roman sat to relieve himself, toga hoisted to his knees, this hole was positioned handily between his legs. Once relief had been achieved, he seized the *xylospongion* by its handle-end, and, by poking it through the front hole, wiped himself clean – without any of his companions having to witness anything more distasteful than a man in a toga bent double and conducting a crude form of keyhole surgery on his own bottom.

Efficient plumbing design ensured that a constant streamlet of waste water from adjoining bath-houses ran through the latrine. So, when the *xylospongion* was done with, it would be dunked and rinsed in the water, and then immersed in a vessel of vinegar, wine or salt-water – ready for the next user.

Hippocrates (circa 460–370 BCE), the ancient world's foremost medical authority, sadly makes very little mention of the *xylospongion* (the term is a sort of cooked-up Greek, ξ λονσπ γγιον, 'wood-sponge'). He was, however, an unrivalled connoisseur of faeces and urine (noting in 400 BCE that the most deadly forms of human stool were 'the black, or fatty, or livid, or verdigris-green, or fetid … those which resemble scrapings, those which are bilious, those resembling leeks …'). He was also no stranger to the nockhole. In one work, he describes the process of performing surgery on haemorrhoids – without anaesthetic, naturally. It's hideous, right from the word 'go' – or, rather, right from the words 'force out

21

the anus as much as possible with the fingers'. But afterwards, Hippocrates provides an insight into the Greeks' equivalent of Preparation H.

In the first instance, the great doctor prescribes a soothing balm of boiled lentils and vetch-seeds. Other remedies include a rinsing with dry wine and the application of sun-dried urine.

(In less severe cases, incidentally, Hippocrates suggests an alternative procedure, far less gruesome, in which the haemorrhoid should be pulled from the anus 'without the patient's knowledge, while he is kept in conversation' – surely a feat of pickpocketing beyond even the most artful dodger).

In the aftermath of the operation, once seven days have passed, Hippocrates at last reaches for the *spongion*:

> Cut a soft sponge into a very slender slice; its width should be about six inches square. Then a thin smooth piece of cloth, of the same size as the sponge, is to be smeared with honey and applied; and with the index finger of the left hand the middle of the sponge is to be pushed as far up as possible; and afterward wool is to be placed upon the sponge so that it may remain in the anus.

'When the patient goes to stool,' Hippocrates adds, 'the part should be washed with hot water.'

Elsewhere in the ancient world, contemplation of the *xylospongion* prompted Martial, a Roman poet of the first century CE, to consider the destiny of his dinner. Addressing a host who sought to curry favour with him by dishing up fine foods (specifically, mullet, hare and pig's udders), Martial concluded:

FROGS, LEEKS AND THUNDER-MUGS

No-one in ancient Greece – in fact, possibly no-one in all human history – has found the act of bum-sponging as funny as the playwright Aristophanes did. Writing in Athens around 405BCE, Aristophanes repeatedly riffed on the Athenians' use of the *spongion*.

In the play *Frogs*, for instance, the god Dionysius, performs rich comic business with the utensil. Demanding a sponge 'for my heart', he in fact ends up wiping his backside with it – explaining that this is where his heart resides, it having been 'frightened, and slunk down into my lower abdomen'.

Meanwhile, *Peace* sees the Athenian Trygaeus use an armoured breastplate as a 'thunder-mug'. He can, explains, use the arm-holes to execute a two-handed wipe.

And in *Plutus*, Aristophanes furnishes an insight into the domestic lives of Athenian slaves: when the slave Carion boasts of his master's new-found wealth, he declares that 'we no longer wipe our arses with stones, but use garlic stalks instead'. For his translation in his alarmingly thorough 1751 *Philosophical Dialogue Concerning Decency*, the lawyer Samuel Rolleston preferred 'leeks' to 'garlic stalks' – but the distinction is probably not worth bickering over, even by the pedantic standards of classical scholars.

It's a fine dinner, very fine, I confess, but tomorrow it will be nothing, or rather today, or rather a moment from now it will be nothing; a matter for a luckless sponge on a doomed mop-stick, or some dog or other, or a crock by the roadside to take care of.

It's a robust approach to restaurant criticism, certainly.

The cultural history of the 'luckless sponge on the doomed mop-stick' – the *infelix damnatae spongia virgae* – took an even darker turn elsewhere in the Empire. The statesman Seneca (d. 65 CE) tells the disturbing tale of a German man, pressed into servitude as a wild-beast gladiator in a Roman amphitheatre. At his training academy one day, the man, during preparations for the next day's 'performance', took leave of his guards to visit the latrine; there, Seneca reports, he 'seized the stick of wood, tipped with a sponge, which was devoted to the vilest uses', and stuffed it down his throat – 'thus he blocked up his windpipe, and choked the breath from his body'.

'It was not a very elegant or becoming way to die,' Seneca comments, 'but what is more foolish than to be over-nice about dying? What a brave fellow!

'The foulest death,' he adds, 'is preferable to the fairest slavery.'

In The Wilderness, Wherein There Is No Bumfodder

Elsewhere in the Empire of the day, perhaps the most notable sub-sect in terms of bathroom conduct were the Essens, or Essenes, who flourished in Palestine between around 200 BCE and 100 CE. The Jewish chronicler Flavius Josephus made a study of their strange practices. According to Josephus, the ascetic Essens lived in communes, eschewed private property and wedlock, and even raised their children communally ('they choose out other persons' children, while they are pliable, and fit for learning, and esteem them to be of their kindred, and form them according to their own manners'). They were devout, restrained in all things, learned, and just.

Taking a closer – if not downright intrusive – look, Josephus noted that the Essens 'think to be sweaty is a good thing'. He was surprised to find that they refused to sit upon a chamber-pot on the Sabbath; equally extraordinarily, they usually disdained chamber-pots on weekdays too, preferring instead a zany alternative procedure:

They dig a small pit, a foot deep, with a paddle (which kind of hatchet is given them when they are first admitted among them); and covering themselves round with their garment, that they may not affront the Divine rays of light, they ease themselves into that pit, after which they put the earth that was dug out again into the pit; and even this they do only in the more lonely places, which they choose out for this purpose; and although this easement of the body be natural, yet it is a rule with them to wash themselves after it, as if it were a defilement to them.

Evidently, the Essens' 'lonely places' were not lonely enough to prevent peeping Josephus from getting an illuminating eyeful.

The Essens' apparent self-disgust with regard to bowel movements marks them out as precursors to those modern-day shy blooms stigmatised by some frank-minded activists as 'shameful shitters' (no, really: Dave Praeger, the curator of the 'Poop Report' website and a campaigner for increased openness on this subject, warns that 'shameful shitting can cause stress, alienation, and [in extreme cases] permanent physical damage'; only by accepting, with Josephus, that *easement of the body be natural* can society 'be freed of the tyranny of the bowel' and 'Pootopia' (again: no, really) be achieved).

But what's really interesting in Josephus' account is his apparent surprise that the Essens should wash themselves after using the toilet. Clearly, there were no established norms for this sort of thing in the ancient world: one might think of the period, in the context of our present enquiries, as a wild dance of innovation and invention, much as we imagine the Renaissance, the Enlightenment, or the Industrial Revolution ...

Or perhaps not. What we are dealing with, after all, is not art or science (and certainly not factory-scale steam power), but only custom – custom, and its all-but-perpetual bedfellow, religion.

In the Islam tradition, the *ahadith* – a collection of stories and sayings attributed to the Prophet Muhammad – are second only to the Qur'an in religious authority. Certain *ahadith* can be seen to represent a typical attempt by religious authority to codify a custom that already exists, albeit in unwarrantedly diverse forms: in this case, the custom is bottom-wiping, and the key *ahadith* can be found in *Kitab Al-Taharah* ('The Book Of Purification') by the ninth-century scholar Muslim ibn al-Hajjaj.

Al-Hajjaj travelled widely in the Islamic world to collect more than three hundred thousand *ahadith* from Iraq, Saudi

Arabia, Syria and Egypt; of these, around four thousand were authenticated and included in his great work, the *Sahih*, one of the six canonical collections of *ahadith*.

In *hadith* #458, the Prophet states that, where a person wipes his bottom with pebbles, he must make use of an odd number of pebbles.

Hadith #460 elaborates: where pebble-wiping occurs, the number of wipes must also be odd. In #504, it is established that the pebbles must not number fewer than three – and that they must not be wielded in the right hand.

Use of the left hand for wiping, and the right for eating and drinking, is endorsed in numerous *ahadith* (Kitab Al-Taharah, for instance, informs us that 'the Prophet ... used his right hand for getting water for ablution and taking food, and his left hand for his evacuation and for anything repugnant). Marco Polo, while sojourning among the peoples of the east, noted: 'They touch not their meat with the left hand, but use only that hand to wipe and other unclean offices.' The seventeenth-century traveller Sir Henry Blount, meanwhile, noted of the people of the Levant (a region corresponding to modern-day Syria, Lebanon, Jordan, Israel and the Palestinian territories) that 'every time they make water, or other unclean exercise of nature, they wash those parts, little regarding who stands by'.

Christian and Jewish scripture, sadly, has no such specific ordinances on the issue of bottom-wiping, the tacit assumption perhaps being that the state of a man's undercarriage is a matter for his own conscience (although the Jewish *halakhah* or traditional law does cover such key topics as talking in the toilet, washing the hands after using the toilet, and eating food in the toilet; in the modern day, considerable debate exists regarding the use of wet-wipes for babies' bottoms on the Sabbath).

As long as the Bible has existed, however, there have existed along with it people who seem unable to resist imposing on its verses their own curious interpretations; this can result in untold horrors, or in rich entertainment. Which brings us back to Samuel Rolleston's *Philosophical Dialogue* of 1751, which falls, without doubt, into the latter category.

St Paul's doleful words in Chapter 4, Verse 13 of 1 Corinthians are rendered in the King James version as: 'We are made as the filth of the world, and are the offscouring of all things unto this day'. Rolleston, however, offers a different translation, and achieves a profound synthesis. 'We are held as despicable as a boghouse sponge,' he writes. 'We are as the bumfodder of all men.'

4. On The Job

'What do you do, if you can't find the loo, in an English country
     garden?
Pull up a leaf and wipe your underneath, in an English country
     garden.'

Traditional English playground song

Coarse vulgarity in the palaces of the mighty is, of course,
distasteful, offensive and highly amusing. But sometimes –
as with many of the other phenomena detailed in this
book – it's only by dropping the niceties that you can get the
job done.

In 1993, Joe Ashton, Labour MP for the mining heartland
of Bassetlaw, Notts, dropped the S-bomb in the House of
Commons during a debate on occupational health and safety.

'There is a saying in the pit that miners, to use biblical
terms, "shit on a shovel",' Ashton told MPs. 'They use coal
dust for their toilet paper, because there is nowhere to wash
their hands.

'What sort of health regulations can there be when there
are no toilets down the coal mines, and nowhere for a man
to wash his hands before he eats his sandwiches during his
break? He simply has to throw what is on the shovel on to

the outbye and let the roof fall in on it. He cannot wash until he gets to the surface and the pithead baths and showers, perhaps three hours later. That is what health and safety is about.'

Labour leader John Smith returned to the theme later the same year, condemning Conservative plans to review the obligation on employers to provide toilet paper in workplace lavatories. 'What kind of uncivilised nonsense are the government engaged in?' Smith demanded.

Similarly grim conditions apparently prevailed among the men who dug out the tunnels of the London Underground. As a tunnel-digger on what would become the Victoria Line in the early nineteen-sixties, the darts player Bobby George recalls that 'you had to wipe your arse on your hand and then wipe your hand on the tunnel wall'. 'It used to stink down there,' George concedes in his autobiography, 'but what could you do?'

You could only do what has always come naturally to workers of every trade and vocation in times of need: when caught short, just do your best.

Sometimes, the choice is made for you. Hunters in the frozen north, such as the *Inuit*, have historically been left without much of a suite of options. If it's summer, scrape up some moss; if it's not, well, then – unless there's a passing lemming you can grab hold of – there's nothing for it but an invigorating handful of snow up the backside.

But the world of work has usually offered a greater range of opportunities than that for the fast-thinking toilet innovator.

One such on-the-job improvisation has earned itself a permanent place in our language. Everyone, from politicians and terrorists to under-fire football managers and reality TV contestants, seems willing – eager, even – to fight on 'to the bitter end'. To take them at their word, if they ever *get* to the bitter end, they might be in for an unpleasant surprise.

Sailors at sea customarily employed the cut end of a ship's rope to, let's say, *swab the decks* after they'd visited the latrine. The rope-end was kept dunked in a bucket of seawater; 'bitter' derives from 'bit', an old word for bucket. As well as a cleansing agent, the sea-water would also act as a cooling below-deck *douche* – much-appreciated during a long haul through the tropics.

No doubt the bitter end played its part in many a below-decks prank. Francis Grose's 1819 *Dictionary Of Slang* records that the jolly tars of the British navy had an uncomplicated sense of humour. In a fun game known as 'The Galley', sailors would shove a 'mopful of excrement' in the face of an unsuspecting landlubber.

Winston Churchill said that there was nothing more to the English naval tradition than rum, sodomy and the lash. He was wrong. There's always been rum, sodomy, the lash, and the bitter end.

Ploughing the ocean wave at least allows the needful latrinist plentiful access to cleansing brine ('water, water, everywhere, nor any drop to drink,' indeed). Back on land, those *actually* ploughing were compelled to find alternatives. Whether closeted in an outhouse or squatting discreetly behind a tree, the key tool in the agricultural toilet-goer's armoury was the corn-cob.

The corn-cob is a powerful symbol of hard life in the rural US – not grilled to a turn and served up with salt and perhaps a knob of butter, but, rather, stripped bare of its corn, dried out, and deployed in a capacity known to precious few other foodstuffs. So iconic is the cob among Americans of a certain class and time that the heavy-drinking writer James Whitcomb Riley ('The Hoosier Poet', 1849–1916) was moved to poetry in its honour.

> The torture of that icy seat
> Would make a Spartan sob,
> For needs must scrape the gooseflesh
> With a lacerating cob.
> That from a frost-encrusted nail
> Was suspended by a string –
> My father was a frugal man
> And wasted not a thing.

The excerpt is from Riley's 'The Passing Of The Outhouse'. It has a claim to being the most eye-watering bit of verse in all American literature.

More recently, 'The Big Wiper' – a fine *nom de plume* for a man following in the steps of the giant Gargantua – put the spirit of scientific inquiry before his own comfort and road-tested the corncob. In a paper posted on the admirably broad-minded Poop Report website (http://www.poopreport.com), the Wiper noted that the dry cob 'felt surprisingly soft' and was 'reasonably absorbent'; in conclusion, he reported that 'corncobs are a viable option, if there are dried corncobs lying around or prepared for this purpose'.

Still, it's hard not to feel that this – when considering the choice of, on the one hand, a dried and comfortless corncob, and, on the other, a kitten-soft roll of modern-day toilet paper – is one circumstance in which Riley's famous lines 'A feeling's ever present/That the Old Times were the best' definitely does not apply.

For rural types in Britain, the *lacerating cob* was, if anything, a distant and terrible rumour from beyond the seas, much like Prohibition or spray-on cheese; the honest British yeoman, if forced to wipe when afield, was more likely to reach for a hank of sheep's wool (the Vikings' bumfodder of choice) or a handful of leaves (British people love leaves, often planting trees outside their houses just so they've got something to rake up in the autumn). The breed or species of leaf, of course, had to be well-chosen, which led to an excellent mediaeval joke:

Q: What is the cleanest leaf in the greenwood?
A: The holly, for no man will wipe his arse upon it.

In between the sailors with their soiled ropes and the farmers with their fistfuls of foliage, we find the people of the seashore – and it's here that we must confront a bottom-cleaning solution that treads a uncertain line between 'innovation' and 'mind-numbing horror'.

Seaweed, you would think, would be the obvious wiping medium for the toilet-going lighthouseman, cockle-picker, fisherman or wrecker. At a pinch, perhaps a patty of moist sand, or some kind of firm, coarsely-scaled sea-fish. But for the coastal folk of the not-too-long-gone past, a starker prospect awaited in the sea-side privy. Shells. Mussel-shells, to be precise.

'I have known an old woman in Holland,' reports Samuel Rolleston in the *Philosophical Dialogue Concerning Decency*, 'set herself on the hole next to a gentleman, and civilly offer him her muscle shell by way of scraper after she had done with it herself.'

One can only hope that they at least chipped the barnacles off them first.

THE HAND THAT HOLDS THE ARSE-WISPE

In addition to those who had to improvise bumfodder while toiling in uncongenial workplaces, history also records the techniques and tools of those whose primary concern was not their own soiled bottoms, but the soiled bottoms of others. Being a page in mediaeval England was a dirty job, but – well, no-one *had* to do it, but plenty did.

The *Babees Book*, dated to the 14th century or thereabouts, was a sort of training manual for children – mostly of noble blood – serving as pages or chamberlains in aristocratic English households. Few details of the job are overlooked. In the chapter that covers the obligations of the young chamberlain in the 'privehouse of esement', we are told, among other things, that the toilet must be covered with green cloth before the Lord assumes his seat. Once the good Lord's business has been completed, the chamberlain should ensure that there is 'blanket, cotyn or lynin' to hand – or, as clarified helpfully in a footnote to an 1868 edition, 'an arse wispe' – for the Lord 'to wipe the nether ende'.

By the beginning of the Tudor period that followed the Wars of the Roses (1455–1485), the role of the man toting towel, jug and arse-wispe had been elevated to one of serious influence, particularly at court. The 'Groom of the Stool' (or 'Close-stool'), in taking responsibility for the king's most intimate procedures, was necessarily a close *confidant* and could act as a trusted advisor; he could even end up guiding the king's policy in matters of the highest importance. The world could be ruled, *pace*

Kipling, not by the hand that rocked the cradle, but the hand that held the arse-wispe.

The Groom of the Stool was the foremost member of the king's privy chamber. According to the historian Dr David Starkey, his influential position was reflected in his status in contemporary society; though he 'had (to our eyes) the most menial tasks', his standing 'was the highest'. The scholar Gail Paster has described the role as 'an exquisite combination of intimacy, degradation and privilege'.

'Clearly then,' Starkey concludes, 'the royal body service must have been seen as entirely honorable, without a trace of the demeaning or the humiliating.' The Groom of the Stool bore 'the indefinable charisma of the monarchy'. This indefinable charisma no doubt had the added benefit of ensuring that the Groom of the Stool got a seat to himself even in the most crowded stagecoach.

The Groom of the Stool achieved his greatest prominence during the reign of Henry VIII (king from 1509 to 1547). Among the men to have assumed this role were William Compton, who resigned from the post in 1526 (but obviously retained royal favour, as he was subsequently granted licence to wear his hat in Henry's presence), and Henry Norris, who was executed in 1536 after being accused of adultery with Anne Boleyn.

Given that the charge against Norris amounted to treason, he was fortunate not to be subjected to the customary punishment for the offence: being hanged, drawn and quartered. But then, perhaps both were preferable to a career spent accompanying the gluttonous and bloated Henry VIII to the toilet.

Perhaps the only way of avoiding this diversity of workplace bumfodder-horrors was to not work at all – to do as a character in the 17th century play *Eastward Hoe* advises, and 'do nothing; be like a gentleman, be idle; the curse of man is labour. Wipe thy bum,' the character urges, 'on testoons.'

A testoon is a kind of Italian coin.

Or maybe the best thing is to keep in mind the message of thirteen-year-old Jasper Ashton-Nelson's winning entry in the 2011 British Young Cartoonist of the Year contest. The cartoon shows a toothbrush moaning: 'I hate my job!' – to which a scowling toilet roll replies: 'You think *yours* is bad?' ...

5. Inky Fingers

'Is this letter written upon Bumf? It looks like it.'

Virginia Woolf, letter to Lytton Strachey, November 1912

'He that Writes abundance of Books, and gets abundance of Children, may in some Sense be said to be a Benefacktor to the public, because he Furnishes it with Bumfodder and Soldiers.' This is No. 124 of Thomas Brown's *Laconics, Or New Maxims Of State And Conversation* (1701). Brown was a raffish Grub Street rascal, a gifted writer, and a prolific and unashamed hack: he may not have fathered any soldiers – at least, any that we know about – but the pages of his voluminous collected works would surely furnish bumfodder enough for all but the most incontinent privy-goer.

In the days before loo-roll, such abuse of the printed page was commonplace. Books, journals and almanacs have long been viewed as a rather luxurious alternative to rags or leaves – or, in the case of the American farmer, corncobs. The Sears & Roebuck mail-order catalogue, first released in 1894, quickly became an outhouse fixture in the rural US – a.k.a. the 'cob and catalogue belt'. Publishers weren't slow to cotton on to this alternative market for their product: Sears & Roebuck's popularity among discerning toilet-goers triggered the production of jocular spin-offs with titles like 'Rears and Sorebutt', and many catalogues of the time were in fact produced with a handy hole in the corner so that the catalogue could easily be hung on a convenient nail.

PUTT'S PRIVIES

Chic Sale's *The Specialist* established him as the Poet Laureate of America's cob and catalogue belt.

Charles 'Chic' Sale, an American comic actor in the nineteen-twenties and thirties, explored the subject in some depth in his 1929 play *The Specialist*. The play – and subsequent book, adapted in order to establish copyright and prevent rival vaudevillians from ripping off Sale's characters – concerns one Lem Putt, an old craftsman who specialises in the construction of privies.

In the first instance, Putt, making plans with a client, establishes a basic principle:

'I can give you a nail or hook for the catalogue, and besides, a box for cobs. You take your pa for instance: he's of the old school and naturally he'd prefer the box; so put 'em both in, Elmer. Won't cost you a bit more for the box and keeps peace in the family. You can't teach an old dog new tricks,' I sez.

Later, though, he moves on to more contemporary issues, and addresses a 'technical point': 'What is the life, or how long will the average mail order catalogue last, in just the plain, ordinary eight family three holer?'

It stumped me for a spell, but this bein' a reasonable question I checked up, and found that by placin' the catalogue in there, say in January – when you get your new one – you should be into the harness section by June; but, of course, that ain't through apple time, and not countin' on too many city visitors, either.

By way of comparison, figures from the modern-day industry indicate that, in the average public toilet, it takes 71.48 separate visits to completely use up a single roll of toilet paper.

But Lem Putt is not done yet:

An' another thing – they've been puttin' so many of those stiff coloured sheets in the catalogue here lately that it makes it hard to figger. Somethin' really ought to be done about this, and I've thought about takin' it up with Mr Sears Roebuck hisself.

The Specialist – despite being only thirty pages long – was an enduring bestseller. 'Chic Sale' even became rural slang for a privy, somewhat to Sale's chagrin.

In the UK, there was no Sears Roebuck, but there was still plenty of bumfodder around for those in need. In her memoir of a 1920s childhood, Diana Holman-Hunt recalls being ordered by her grandmother to make herself useful by cutting a stack of 'circulars, envelopes and paper bags' into sheets of toilet-paper.

'Some of these bags from Palmer's Stores are very thick and covered with writing,' she observes with concern.

'Print is all right on one side, you know,' is her pragmatic grandmother's response.

The young Miss Holman-Hunt is resourceful enough to ensure that the chore is not without its perks:

When I had cut a hundred sheets, I pierced their corners and threaded them with a string; I tied this in a loop to hang on a nail by the 'convenience'. I made a mental note of the softer pieces and put them together in the middle, between the back of a calendar from Barkers and an advertisement for night-lights.

A wartime equivalent was lampooned in the BBC's World War One-set sitcom *Blackadder Goes Forth* in 1989, in which the soldiers' propaganda paper *King & Country* – 'damned inspiring stuff', according to the idealistic Lieutenant George – is praised by the cynical Captain Blackadder as 'soft, strong and thoroughly absorbent' (to which General Melchett replies, 'Yes, I thought it would be right up your alley').

In all such cases, the wiper's comfort comes first – and the finer feelings of the proud author be damned.

In fact, the finer feelings of the proud author have in many cases been not merely collateral damage but, rather, the vengeful wiper's intended target. Participants in the no-holds-barred festival of envy, spite and malice that we know fondly as the literary *demimonde* have seldom scrupled to strike this lowest and dirtiest of blows.

The Latin poet Catullus, for instance, was apparently prepared to eschew the briny *xylospongion* in favour of a fistful of a rival's verse when there were scores to be settled. 'Come you here into the fire, you bundle of rusticity and clumsiness, chronicle of Volusius, filthy waste-paper,' he writes in his Poem 36 – although 'filthy waste-paper', in FW Cornish's genteel Edwardian version, may be a less faithful translation of Catullus's *cacata carta* than something along the lines of 'defecated papers'. What Volusius had done to deserve such opprobrium is not recorded.

Sometimes, the creation of *defecated papers* can seem not only contemptuous but downright ungrateful. In one of his celebrated *colloquia*, the 16th-century Dutch humanist Erasmus sets down a dialogue in which one character demands: 'I had rather receive Money than Letters … What advantage do empty Letters bring? … To whom are Letters grateful or acceptable without Money?' – to which comes the reply: 'They are useful, fit, proper, to wipe your Breech with. They are good to wipe your Backside with. If you don't know the use of them, they are good to wipe your Arse with.'

Not a man you'd want as a pen-pal.

INSULTS AND ARSE-WISPES

SWIFT WASN'T THE ONLY ONE WITH A TASTE FOR
WIPEBREECH-THEMED ABUSE ...

WOLFGANG AMADEUS MOZART

Mozart often used his bottom as rhetorical short-hand to
express contempt. Had he not others beside himself to think
of, he wrote to his father in 1780, he would use his contract
with the archiepiscopal court of Salzburg 'to wipe my arse'.

JOHN DRYDEN

The poet John Dryden (1631–1700) took a withering swipe
at Grub Street bumfodder-merchants in his 1676 epic 'Mac
Flecknoe' (the poem's specific target was Dryden's bitter foe
Thomas Shadwell):

> From dusty shops neglected authors come,
> Martyrs of pies, and reliques of the bum.

In the poem, the poet Shadwell is characterised as the 'hoary prince' of these writers of verse fit only for lining pie-dishes and cleansing backsides.

CARAVAGGIO

In turn-of-the-17th-century Rome, Michelangelo Merisi – better known as Caravaggio, the name he took from his Lombardy home-town – earned fame not only as a painter but as a swordsman, troublemaker and, ultimately, murderer. In 1603 he turned to the poetical form of the *pasquinade* (a kind of bawdy satirical poem) to hit out at his loathed rival, the painter Giovanni Baglioni:

> Therefore take
> Your drawings and cartoons
> That you have made, to Andrea the grocer's shop
> [so that Andrea could wrap groceries with them]
> Or wipe your arse with them
> Or ...

The next line is simply too rude for words.

JOHN OLDHAM

The poet John Oldham, a contemporary of Dryden, appeared depressed by the fact that his work seemed doomed to meet its end at the end of another. In his 'Satyr' (1683), Oldham is visited by the ghost of the Elizabethan poet Edmund Spenser. Poetry, the mournful ghost laments, has grown debased, and poets enjoy less esteem among the public than scandalous celebrities. And ultimately, Spenser's shade foretells, 'Who'll not laugh to see ... all thy deathless Monuments of Wit/ Wipe Porters Tails or mount in Paper Kite?'.

Robert Herrick

Herrick (1591–1674) was alert to the danger of his verse being put to uses other than those for which they were intended. In a cautionary preface entitled 'To His Booke', he placed a curse on anyone who mistook his poetry for bumfodder:

> Who with thy leaves shall wipe (at need)
> The place, where swelling Piles do breed:
> May every ill, that bites, or smarts,
> Perplex him in his hinder parts.

Perhaps the most gifted of all the writers who have added the barbed wipe to their armoury of satirical weapons is the greatest satirist of them all: Jonathan Swift (1667–1745), Dean of St Patrick's cathedral, Dublin. Not for nothing did Coleridge call him 'the soul of Rabelais dwelling in a dry place'; Voltaire, similarly, called him 'Rabelais sober'.

Such was Swift's virtuosity in this field that he was able to extend his range beyond bad literature to incorporate practically any kind of printed matter. If someone could publish it, Swift could find a way to talk about someone wiping their arse with it. In his 'A Poem On High Church', Swift details the after-effects of the 'dose of cant-fail' prescribed to the non-conformist churchmen (as will be seen, toilet humour retains its bite even when time has rendered the political satire somewhat obsolete):

It purges the spleen
Of dislike to the queen,
And has one effect that is odder;
When easement they use,
They always will chuse
The Conformity Bill for bumfodder.

But Swift didn't stop at Acts of Parliament. Next on the roll for the Dean was the innocent (and, one would think, impracticably tiny) ballot-paper. His 'A Character, Panegyric, And Description Of The Legion Club' is a savage assault on the corrupt Irish Parliament – and includes the deployment of Swift's trademark dirty protest:

Let them, with their gosling quills,
Scribble senseless heads of bills;
We may, while they strain their throats,
Wipe our a——s with their votes.

Aficionados of scatological satire might also enjoy, from the same poem, 'Dear companions, hug and kiss,/Toast Old Glorious in your piss' and 'Gallows Carter, Dilks, and Clements,/Souse them in their own excrements'.

But the use of wipe-breech as literary critique was not considered universally to be in the best taste.

Friedrich Dedekind's 1558 poem *Grobianus* is a lavishly revolting epic of bad manners, covering every aspect of dinner-table etiquette, from the first principles of quaffing and gorging to the finer points of urinating, vomiting and groping one's neighbour. By 1609, the English scholar and playwright Thomas Dekker felt that *Grobianus* was in need of updating, the better to reflect modern manners. His *Gul's Horne-Book* is a bawdy manual for the 17th-century gallant-about-town, and includes a fascinating snippet on post-prandial table talk – that is, what to say to your fellow diners on returning from the 'close-stool'.

Being returned again to the board, you shall sharpen the wits of all the eating gallants about you and do them great pleasure to ask what pamphlets or poems a man might think fittest to wipe his tail with; (marry, this talk will be somewhat foul, if you carry not a strong perfume about you;) and, in propounding this question, you may abuse the works of any man; deprave his writings that you cannot equal; and purchase to yourself in time the terrible name of a severe critic.

Not all experts on etiquette have viewed such usage as a mortal insult to the author – some, on the contrary, have considered it a sincere compliment.

The unbearably proper Lord Chesterfield (1694–1773) spent years obsessively tutoring his unfortunate son Philip in 'the necessary arts of the world'. No detail of conduct was too minor to merit a mention in Chesterfield's lengthy letters (he was prolific as well as pedantic: by the time of Philip's death at the age of thirty-six, the letters numbered four hundred and forty-eight). In a 1747 epistle, Chesterfield explains to his son how one can ensure that time spent in the 'necessary house' is profitably spent.

I know a gentleman, who was so good a manager of his time, that he would not even lose that small portion of it, which the calls of nature obliged him to pass in the necessary-house; but gradually went through all the Latin poets, in those moments. He bought, for example, a common edition of Horace, of which he tore off gradually a couple of pages, carried them with him to that necessary place, read them first, and then sent them down as a sacrifice to Cloacina: this was so much time fairly gained; and I recommend you to follow his example. It is better than only doing what you cannot help doing at those moments; and it will make any book, which you shall read in that manner, very present in your mind.

Chesterfield, in dispensing this helpful advice, was unwittingly echoing a nobleman of an earlier age and rather more ribald disposition. The naval officer Sir John Mennes, with his like-minded clergyman friend Dr James Smith, published *Musarum Deliciae, or the Muses Recreations* in 1656. Both writers were heavy drinkers, riotous livers and all-round gadabouts (one biography of Mennes describes him as 'something of a sexual connoisseur, candid about buggery, teasing about bestiality, though with a personal preference for the simple charms of the women of Bury St Edmunds'). In *Musarum Deliciae*, they describe a trip to take the waters at the Epsom spa – and express their dismay upon finding what other visitors have been using for toilet-paper.

But then the pity to behold
Those antient Authors, which of old
Wrote down for us, Philosophy,
Physick, Music, and Poetry;

Now to no other purpose tend
But to defend the fingers end.

The facetious poets go on to list the writers of antiquity whose works have been thus spoiled:

Here lies *Romes Naso* torn and rent,
Now reeking from the fundament;
. . .
Here did lye *Virgil*, there lay *Horace*,
Which newly had wip'd his, or her arse.
Anacreon reeled to and fro,
Vex'd, that they used his papers so.
And *Tully* with his Offices,
Was forc'd to do such works as these.

And it was not only classical literature that Mennes and Smith found lying around in a state of embumfment: the 'Letter of a Lover' and 'Sonnets halfe written' had also been forced to obey necessity.

A similar business was later encapsulated somewhat more pithily in an anonymous limerick:

There was a young fellow named Chivy
Who, whenever he went to the privy,
First solaced his mind,
Then wiped his behind,
With some well-chosen pages of Livy.

Wiping as a means of improving the mind was also proposed – albeit with tongue firmly in cheek – by the Wakefield-born doctor John Radcliffe in the 17th century. A hypochondriac nobleman who had befriended Radcliffe was complaining to him of hearing 'singing noises' in his head; 'If it be so,' the plain-speaking Radcliffe reportedly replied, 'I can prescribe to your Lordship no other remedy than that of swiping your arse with a ballad.' According to a contemporary source, the response 'perfectly cured his Lordship's malady'.

But it should be remembered that one man's *torchecul* may be another man's treasure. In the late 19th century, a copy of William Caxton's *Recuyell of the Hystoryes of Troye* – one of the earliest printed books in English – was sold for thirty pounds to a Manchester book-dealer. It had been found hanging on a nail in a Harrogate water-closet.

(Caxton also printed a version of Chaucer's *Canterbury Tales*, which would have made a far better bog-side companion than the *Recuyell*, being stuffed as it is with farts and arseholes – not to mention a 'shitten shepherd', who by the sound of it could use a wipedown himself – perhaps with wool from one of his 'clene shepe').

But the connotations of wiping with writing remain – to say the least – more negative than positive. Perhaps the most well-known (and widely mis-attributed) expression of the spiteful wiper's sentiment is the famous riposte to a hostile critic: 'I am sitting in the smallest room of my house. I have your review before me. In a moment it will be behind me.'

This glorious dismissal has been attributed variously to Voltaire, HL Mencken and (inevitably) George Bernard Shaw – actually, it was penned in 1906 by the German composer Max Reger, in response to Rudolph Louis, critic for the *Muchner Neuste Nachrichten*.

But it's one thing when an individual's feelings are hurt by such dirty work; it's quite another when an entire nation is so impugned.

DEFILING THE FLAG

It's one thing when an individual's feelings are hurt by this kind of dirty work, it's quite another when an entire nation is so impunged . . .

Documents from 1840 report that, in the port of Freetown, Sierra Leone, a British officer, rudely boarding the French ship *L'Aigle*, was told that he would not dare to act so offensively if there were a French man-o'-war in the vicinity – to which the Brit, showing all the famed tact and grace of the English officer class, replied that, 'if he had the flag of the French nation, he would wipe his arse with it'. Fortunately, he had no such flag to hand, and so the outrage was averted.

In 2010, however, the outrage was not only perpetrated – it was caught on camera. A special prize in a photography contest organised in the French city of Nice by retailer FNAC was awarded to a striking image of a man using the cherished *tricolore* to wipe his bottom (the feat seems particularly impressive in view of the fact that the flag was still attached to its flagpole). A furore, predictably, followed.

'I want whoever committed this outrage to be penalised, and possibly those who published [the photo] too,' raged Eric Ciotti, president of the Alpes-Maritime regional council.

Justice Minister Michele Alliot-Marie agreed, calling for the criminal prosecution of those responsible. A spokesperson for the justice department added: 'If the current law proves to be unsatisfactory on this point, then it should be changed.'

But it's very difficult to use the law to prevent dissidents from wiping their bums on flags if they're determined to do so. Even the US, which officially regards the Stars and Stripes as 'a living thing', ultimately decided that its Flag Code – which insists that the flag should never be 'used ... in such a manner as to permit it to be easily ... soiled', thus ruling out bumfoddery – was not legally enforceable under the terms of the US Constitution's First Amendment.

There was clearly no such constitutional right in place in twelfth-century Austria: Richard I (the Lionheart) was banged up in a dungeon by the Arch-duke of Austria for throwing the country's flag down a privy.

Flags are not the only national emblems to have been pressed into unseemly toilet service: many a backpacker's anecdote begins with the teller finding himself in a squalid hole-in-the-floor latrine with no bumfodder to hand but a pocketful of local banknotes, and ends with the punchline: 'The *rupee* [or *baht*, or *ringgit*, or *kyat*] was certainly deval- ued that day ...'

There are other ways in which bum-wiping can lead to ille- gal levels of disrespect. The advent of toilet-paper (of which more later) has combined with certain quirks of the English national character to create an interesting inversion of the traditional procedure. No longer is it necessary to use con- temptible documentation *as* toilet paper; it is much more convenient – and comfortable – to express disdain by writing *on* toilet paper. This is the root of what seems to have become one of the many minor traditions of the incorrigibly odd English courtroom.

In 1981, one Mr Malcolm Hancock of Swindon, England, was fined the sum of twenty pounds for the offence of making a right turn at a 'No Right Turn' sign. 'As was his right, as a Britisher,' his MP, David (later Lord) Stoddart, later explained, 'he thought that the penalty was inordinately great.'

To register his disgust – and forge his own small but memorable place in the history of the Little Man Who Wouldn't Lie Down – Mr Hancock wrote out a cheque for the stipulated sum on a sheet of toilet paper (quite a feat of craftsmanship, one would imagine). It was, according to David Stoddart, 'a very reasonable piece of toilet paper'. Mr Hancock took the precaution of consulting both his solicitor and his bank manager, both of whom confirmed the validity of the cheque, and made his payment to the court. The letter of the law had not been breached; its spirit had been deftly and satisfyingly pooh-poohed.

Sadly, Mr Hancock's satisfaction was short-lived. Within days, a troop of policemen turned up at his house. He was arrested, slung into the cells, and kept there for nineteen hours.

David Stoddart's presentation of Mr Hancock's case to the House of Commons in April 1981 can only be described as magnificent. He had, he said, reported the pettiness of the clerk of the Swindon magistrates' court to both the Home Secretary and the Lord Chancellor. The Home Secretary had not replied; the Lord Chancellor, however, had written Mr Stoddart 'a letter that made all sorts of suggestions against my constituent. He even suggested that my constituent had insulted Her Majesty. But Mr. Hancock is the most ardent royalist.'

Building to a climax, Stoddart declared: 'I regret that Her Majesty has been brought into this issue. She has not only a sense of humour but the wisdom to ensure that such incidents do not result in subjects being arrested and incarcerated for 19 hours. She has too much wisdom for that.

'In addition,' he went on, 'Her Majesty has good business sense and knows that when any form of money is offered it should be accepted with alacrity and placed in the bank or spent on a good cause.'

In conclusion, Stoddart expressed his hope that, 'by bringing this matter to the attention of the House, we shall get more circumspect actions by the clerk to the Swindon magistrates' court and that it will be made clear to him that Parliament does not approve of his oppressive attitude.'

Sadly, the might of Parliament was never brought to bear on the officious Wiltshire clerk. But this was not the last time that such Andrex cheques would feature in urgent questions in the House. In 1982, Labour MP Christopher Price demanded of the then Attorney General, Michael Havers, whether he was familiar with the case of a man who had been imprisoned for submitting a cheque written on the carcase of a dead rat – 'on the ground that his house was rat-infested, and he wanted to draw attention to that fact.'

With all the grave dignity of his office, Havers replied: 'With regard to the use of unusual documents for cheques, I have heard only of toilet paper being used. This is the first time that I have heard of a dead rat being used'.

Writing on loo-roll, though, need not be a sign of contempt. In at least one instance, it has been a rather sweet romantic gesture.

VD Nabokov, the father of the novelist Vladimir, was a reformist liberal under the restrictive rule of Tsar Nicholas II. In 1904, one anti-Tsar gesture too many led to Nabokov being sentenced to three months' solitary confinement. During his imprisonment, he still managed to keep in touch with his wife, Elena – smuggling out letters to her written on sheets of toilet paper.

6. Paper Pushers

'Who his foul tail with paper wipes,
Shall at his ballocks leave some chips.'

Gargantua & Pantagruel, Book I

The foregoing chapter might have given the misleading impression that the wipers of the past wouldn't deign to clean themselves with paper unless it had something printed on it – as though printers' ink were some kind of desirable emollient, like aloe vera. This was not, of course, the case. Pages from books and catalogues simply happened to be the only sort of paper one generally had lying about the (out)house.

In the modern age, literature is usually deployed as bum-fodder only in an emergency (as in 2012, when the singer Solange Knowles – sister of the megastar Beyoncé – reported being 'Out of gas. Stranded in the Texas desert. Had to pee by the railroad. Wiped with pages of *The Great Gatsby*.'). We now have specialist wiping matter, developed specifically for the purpose.

For what we in the modern-day west might provincially call Proper Toilet Paper, we have one man to thank: Joseph Gayetty, America's out-house Edison.

(Actually, there may have been a British fore-runner to Gayetty: an Elisha Gay to his Alexander Graham Bell, a Liebnitz to his Newton. GW Atkins & Co, prominent in the 1890s, claimed to have held a royal warrant for the production of toilet paper since 1817).

Gayetty was a New York-based entrepreneur who dared to dream of a future free of unsympathetic torn-out Sears catalogue pages. In 1857 – well before Edison's lightbulb or Benz's internal-combustion engine – Gayetty's medicated toilet paper hit the shops. At stores like John F Henry's Great United States Family Medicine Warehouse (No. 8, College Place, New York), it joined such products as Upham's Hair Gloss, Kellinger's Liniment and Saratoga 'A' Water on the groaning shelves.

It would be nice to think that Gayetty's brainwave arrived somewhat along the lines of that experienced by Archimedes, a man who also reached new heights of inspiration while in the bathroom: 'while the [matter of calculating the volume of irregularly-shaped objects] was still on his mind, he happened to go to the bath, and on getting into a tub observed that the more his body sank into it the more water ran out over the tub,' the architect Vitruvius reported in about 15 BCE. 'Without a moment's delay, and transported with joy, he jumped out of the tub and rushed home naked, crying with a loud voice that he had found what he was seeking; for as he ran he shouted repeatedly in Greek, "Ευρηκα, ευρηκα" [*Eureka, eureka* – I have it, I have it]'. We don't know whether Joseph Gayetty leapt up from the toilet with just the same excited alacrity as Archimedes leapt from the bath – but, in the absence of evidence to the contrary, we might as well imagine that he did.

Gayetty's Medicated Paper was impregnated with aloe and sold at 50 cents per pack of five hundred sheets; each sheet was 21 by 14 centimetres, a little larger than the dimensions of the average paperback book. It was, the blurb announced, 'unbleached pearl-colored pure manila hemp paper'. Gayetty had stern words for those thinking of sticking with old newspaper or catalogues. 'Printer's ink is a rank poison,' the packaging warned, 'and a persistive use of printed paper is sure eventually to induce an aggravated stage of [haemorrhoids].'

In a bold marketeering move, he had his name printed as a watermark on every sheet.

The *New Orleans Medical News and Hospital Gazette* responded swiftly – and scornfully. In its April 1859 issue, the *Gazette* published an article under the heading: 'QUACKERY.'

The piece bemoaned the 'horde of lung doctors, pile doctors, corn doctors, biologists, phrenologists, electricians [sic]' who besieged the city of New Orleans during the winter months in order to prey on 'the miserable credulity of mankind'.

'But there is no use inveighing against them,' the *Gazette*'s correspondent sighed. 'Rather let us amuse ourselves over THE LATEST QUACK ADVERTISEMENT.'

What nefarious snake-oil salesman might the *Gazette* be referring to? Some madcap chiropractor? A crackpot homeopath? It could have been the former, but not the latter (homeopathy had been going since the 1790s, but in 1859 chiropractic pioneer DD Palmer was barely a teenager, and some way away from his encounter with the ghostly physician Dr Jim Atkins (deceased) and his subsequent thesis that '95 per cent of all diseases are caused by displaced vertebrae, the remainder by luxation of other joints'). In fact, it was neither. It was, as you will have guessed, the celebrated Mr Gayetty.

'Homoeopathy, hydropathy, *et id homne genus* [the learned gents of the *Gazette* presumably meant *et id genus omne*, 'and everything of that sort'] must now hide their diminished heads,' the journal sneered. 'Mr Gayetty of New York City has found that the public mind is prepared for anything whatever in the shape of humbuggery, and he at once, with true Yankee readiness, administers to their rapacious appetites in a manner to be admired, if humbuggery is ever admirable.'

What follows is a masterpiece of patrician condescension (in spite of the sly bottom-related puns):

> Inasmuch as this idea of Mr Gayetty is strictly a fundamental one, it must be valuable, and we cannot resist the temptation to "give him a lift" in our pages. We, therefore, insert his advertisement in full, as we clip it from the *National Intelligencer* (!!), with one suggestion, viz., that he not only places his autograph on each sheet of his invaluable paper, to prevent counterfeit, but that he furnishes his millions of patrons with his photograph in like manner. More, we suggest that the photograph be taken with a bland smile on the face. We are really anxious to see the face of the man who is going to eclipse even homoeopathy in the inestimable benefits he thus rubs into mankind; and then, again, it would be such a capital idea to be thus cheering up the sufferer by smiling on the very seat of his troubles. The cheerful countenance of Mr Gayetty would be worth the small price of the paper. *Oh tempora! Oh mores!*

In this last instance, the author's classical education had not let him down; the phrase, from Cicero, translates as 'Oh, the times!, Oh, the manners!'.

(Hastening to back up the *Gazette* was the *Medical And Surgical Reporter*, which reprinted the *Gazette*'s attack with the ribald prologue: 'Empiricism has changed tactics. Its usual bold effrontery is turned to attack the public in the rear. Mr Gayetty of New York intends to take advantage of them by catching them with their breeches down.')

Gayetty became the *Gazette*'s byword for weak-minded mountebankery. In 1860, it issued a statement to the Boston patent-medicine producer Tilden & Co, which had continued to send advertisements to be printed in the journal in spite of the journal's avowed contempt.

'We would rather stitch the advertisement of Gayetty's medicated paper for the water closet under our cover,' the *Gazette* declared grandly, 'than the sheets they send us. The medicated paper can do no harm, and we have no idea that the originator of it aspires to any other title than that of quack; while these manufacturers of spurious compound cathartic pills and fermenting extracts have extensively preyed upon the credulity of the profession and inflicted infinite injury on suffering humanity.'

The original advertisement that so provoked the *Gazette* to such heights of withering contempt is not only a classic of its kind but also a strikingly prescient bit of fortune-telling:

Misery Obviated – The greatest blessing of the age is JC Gayetty's Medicated Paper for the Water-closet. It is endorsed by the press, the clergy, the bar the school-teacher, the merchant, the family and the public generally.

To use the language of one of the New York dailies: 'It is beautiful pure Manilla paper, as delicate as a bank-note, and as stout as foolscap, entirely divested of the poisonous chemicals of so-called pure white paper, and of printer's ink, and is medicated so as to cure and prevent piles. The medication is perfect, acquired by a process for which the discoverer has taken out a patent.

'It is harmless to healthy persons, and a luxury into the bargain. It is warranted, let us repeat, to cure and prevent piles. It is a household hold comfort. It will become a popular necessity.'

Within a few years, Gayetty's medicated had crossed the Atlantic, and its antiseptic whiff had piqued the sensibilities of the esteemed publishers of *The Lancet*, Britain's premier medical publication. British doctors were dismissive of the new consumer gimmick that sought to replace a field of medicine that dated back to Hippocrates himself.

Here is the latest absurdity. We have received from a correspondent a circular advocating the advantages to be derived from the use of a medicated paper in the cure of hemorrhoids. The inventor has a high opinion of his discovery; for he anticipates that "this article will be found in the household of every refined man in the kingdom". He attributes the production of piles to the use of printed and ordinary paper, especially white paper.

As this cause is not noticed in the works of those who write on that subject, it might be of use to the surgeons who take the rectal region under their care to know that the prognosis, pathology, and therapeutics of this malady are simplified in an uncommon degree, and that their occupation is now gone to the Wall. All that is required is a simple piece of paper with the name "Gayetty" stamped on it, guaranteed both to prevent and cure the complaint. The circular, written in excellent taste, and posted in such a way as to be received at breakfast – with *private* on the envelope outside – will be sure to harmonise with the feelings of many sufferers at that time.

We won't dwell on who had the last laugh here.

The Bumfodder That Dare Not Speak Its Name

Not all of Gayetty's rivals in the emergent toilet-paper market were as unembarrassed as the inspired JC. The Scott Company, for example, was so bashful about its name appearing on its toilet-paper packs that it instead specialised in creating customised products for its customers. The long-running 'Waldorf' brand is one such product, dating back to a deal with a New York merchant in 1902. British firms, perhaps surprisingly, seem to have been less reticent, and more inclined to take the view that even bumf-based publicity is good publicity: in addition to the widely used 'Council Property' and 'Government Property' stamps, toilet rolls in the UK carried such iconic names as Barclays Bank, National Coal Board, London School of Economics (for those who like to sit down with a pencil and work it out), Associated British Cinemas and even the United Kingdom Atomic Energy Authority.

But across the pond, shoppers continued to approach the purchase of a toilet-roll in the shifty, furtive manner of a fourteen-year-old buying his first copy of *Penthouse*.

'No conversation,' one advert for Scott's ScotTissue murmured reassuringly, 'just say "ScotTissue" to your storekeeper and receive a big, economical, dustproof roll.' Hakle also traded on the shamefulness of its product: 'Ask for a roll of Hakle,' its ads urged, 'and then you don't have to mention toilet paper!' Many shoppers acquired the habit of simply asking for 'two, please', so as to avert the horror of naming That Which Must Not Be Named.

The publications on which most US business relied for advertising were similarly shy on toilet-related subjects: the first loo-roll ad didn't appear until 1890, and even that was only a single, small image of a package of paper (not a word of advertising copy was permitted) in the *Atlantic Monthly*.

A similar degree of tact and discretion was required of William Whewell, the master of Trinity College, Cambridge, when, on a visit to the university, Queen Victoria betrayed her ignorance of this latest development in bum-hygiene. Crossing the filthy river Cam, into which all manner of effluent was routinely discharged, the stately monarch pointed to the water and asked: 'What are all those little pieces of paper?'

With impressive presence of mind, Whewell replied: 'Those, ma'am, are notices that bathing is forbidden.'

It was probably around this time – with gentility increasingly rivalling cleanliness for next-to-godliness status – that one of the more curious toilet paper adjuncts first came into fashion. Like many of the products in this history, it filled a niche in the market that most right-minded people would never have recognised as needing to be filled; it's fair to say that, if the toilet-roll cosy did not exist, it would not be necessary to invent it.

In *The Meaning Of Liff*, John Lloyd and Douglas Adams' helpful dictionary of words there aren't any words for yet, the authors name their new coinages using 'words that aren't doing anything other than hanging around on signposts'. Thus, a small West Yorkshire town lends its name to 'a frilly spare-toilet-roll-cosy': Lloyd and Adams call it an *ossett* (equally usefully, 'The barely soiled sheet of toilet paper which signals the end of the bottom-wiping process' is named as a *riber*).

The typical 20th-century incarnation of this bathroom design classic is in the form of a doll whose voluminous skirts conceal a shameful secret: *a spare loo roll.*

In the earliest days of toilet-paper concealment, though, paper didn't come in a convenient roll, and so decorators had to be more ingenious in how they kept evidence of their disgraceful toilet practices hidden from the prying eyes of guests and plumbers. One particularly charming example was 'Madam's Double Utility Fan', which had a hidden compartment in its handle (pay attention, 007) containing one hundred and fifty sheets of toilet paper cut to fit the fan's shape.

Loo-roll privacy remains a pressing concern for many, even in these candid modern times. 'Sometimes it's hard to hide those unsightly spare toilet paper rolls,' sighs an ad for one modern-day ossett retailer. These same retailers are responsible for what is surely the only use of the adjective 'romantic' in any form of toilet-roll-related advertising – as in, 'Why not add a romantic Victorian touch to your bathroom decor?...' – and are presumably the modern-day equivalents of the target market for the 1950s Charmin slogan: 'If you're the kind of person who brightens her home with flowers, you'll prefer Charmin tissue!'

As the Victorian Age of Invention hastened on, it was either the Scott Company or the Albany Perforated Wrapping Paper Company that took the next giant leap – playing Henry Ford to Gayetty's Benz – and produced perforated paper in the form of convenient rolls (the relevant patent is in the name of Albany's Seth Wheeler, and dated to 1871). In Britain, the market leader was WW Colley & Co. of Hatton Garden, London, patent-holders for terebene-infused perforated paper (terebene is a colourless chemical, widely used as an expectorant). At the Paris *Exposition Universelle* of 1899 – an eclectic show that also featured Buffalo Bill Cody's wild west show and the largest diamond in the world – Colley's paper was awarded a gold medal; Colley rolls were used in all the lavatories at the *Exposition*, including those in the brand-new (and widely disliked) Eiffel Tower.

Perforation is a technological breakthrough that has been

largely – but not entirely – overlooked by cultural commentators. But in his 1988 novel *The Mezzanine*, Nicholson Baker paid an appropriate tribute, as his narrator contemplates the workings of the paper dispenser in his corporate toilet cubicle:

> Perforation! Shout it out! The deliberate punctuated weakening of paper and cardboard so that it will tear along an intended path, leaving a row of fine-haired white pills or tuftlets on each new edge! It is a staggering conception, showing an age-transforming feel for the unique properties of pulped wood fiber. Yet do we have national holidays to celebrate its development?

Inexplicably, we do not. The narrator goes on to demand:

> Why isn't the pioneer of perforation chiseled into the façades of libraries, along with Locke, Franklin, and the standard bunch of French Encyclopedists? They would have loved him!

Not everyone shares this enthusiasm: some Orthodox Jews refuse to tear toilet-paper along its perforations on the Sabbath, opting to use a foot or elbow to do the tearing instead.

Anyway, the perforated roll was to usher in a new era of toilet-driven consumerism. In 1880s Philadelphia, the Scotts led the market; in London at around the same time, WJ Alcock started selling rolls under the Bronco brand (Bronco remained the dominant brand until the 1950s, and many Britons still can't hear the name without emitting an involuntary whimper).

This was the period during which the monsters – or, perhaps, the dinosaurs – of the industry established themselves.

Kimberly, Clark & Company was established in the city of Neenah, Wisconsin, in the 1870s (Neenah's other main claim to fame is its use in the title of the song 'Where The Hell Is Neenah?' by the band Cheeseheads With Attitude). Its founders – John A. Kimberly and Charles B. Clark (the businessmen) and Havilah Babcock and Frank C. Shattuck (the salesmen) – pooled the sum of $30,000 (in retrospect, given K-C's position as a toilet market-leader, it seems a pity that the firm was named after Kimberly and Clark, and not their two co-investors). Their Atlas Mill began manufacturing newspaper from cotton rags in October 1872; a couple of years later, they took over Neenah's other mill, establishing a local monopoly.

With a group of other investors, Kimberly, Clark & Co. founded the Atlas Paper Company in 1878. Their principal product was wrapping paper. In 1881, they opened a new mill, naming it Vulcan (after, presumably, the Roman god of fire, rather than the race of pointy-eared logicians) and turning it over to the production of book paper. By the mid-1880s, the firm – having settled on the name Kimberly & Clark – was the biggest paper manufacturer in the midwest.

1888 brought a setback, when the Atlas Mill burned down – by the firm quickly set about building a replacement, hiring the architect A.B. Tower (described by John A. Kimberly as 'the prince of paper-mill architects').

Charles B. Clark, the youngest of the firm's founding fathers, died in 1891 at the age of 47, but things were looking up for Mr Shattuck and Mr Babcock, who finally got something named after them when the firm's Shattuck & Babcock mill was built in DePere, Wisconsin. It was Frank Shattuck's last triumph: he died in 1901, the same year that another mill fire threatened to ruin the company he had helped to found. In 1905, Havilah Babcock, too, passed on – only John Kimberly was left standing.

As the ageing Kimberly gradually withdrew from the company's business, the firm – now Kimberly-Clark – came under the *de facto* control of director Frank J. Sensenbrenner. In 1914, another new face came into the picture: Ernst Mahler, a young scientist who was appointed to run K-C's new research and development lab. On a tour of brink-of-war Europe with company heir James Kimberly, Mahler unlocked the secrets of two processes that would be key to the company's future direction: bleached refined groundwood printing paper, and creped cellulose wadding (no, it's not exactly splitting the atom – but then, you can't wipe your bum on an atom, split or otherwise).

Kimberly-Clark's 'Cellucotton' was used in bandages for wounded soldiers during the first World War, and – just as the war came to an end in 1918 – was investigating its possible use as a filter for army gas masks (the project was shelved following the Armistice, but only temporarily – these studies laid the groundwork for the firm's future development of Kleenex tissues).

The firm's first steps in the field of embarrassing personal hygiene products were concerned not with toilet paper but with sanitary napkins; Kimberly-Clark's Kotex brand was advertised with Art Deco illustrations of elegant, sophisticated women – and was sold under the counter in unmarked brown-paper packages.

The year 1928 brought an era to an end: John A. Kimberly died, and Frank Sensenbrenner was named president. The following year, the Kimberly-Clark Corporation was launched on the New York Stock Exchange – just in time for the Wall Street Crash.

Strong sales of Kleenex tissues saw Kimberly-Clark safely through the Depression. The firm was still skirting the growing toilet-roll market, although it did diversify its product range quite significantly in the 1940s: US soldiers in the second World War made use of Kimberly-Clark machine-gun mounts and detonating fuses.

In the 1950s, Kimberly-Clark set up its first bases outside the US, opening plants in Mexico and the UK. In 1960 the firm again went to war, supplying surgical fabrics for military surgeons in Korea.

Throughout the 1970s and 80s, the firm showed a growing interest in poo-related products – cornering the market in both disposable nappies and adult incontinence pants – without yet biting the bullet and moving into the T.P. sector. That had to wait until 1995, when, following months of negotiation, Kimberly-Clark merged with a fellow paper giant: the Scott Company.

THE SCOTT COMPANY

The Scott brothers of Philadelphia – Thomas, Irvin and Clarence – has established their paper commission company in June 1874, in partnership with their cousins Thomas Seymour and Zerah Hoyt. However, hard times during the 1870s forced the firm out of business. But Irvin and Clarence were not to be discouraged. Irvin borrowed two thousand dollars from his father-in-law, and by 1879 the Scott Paper Company, after an inauspicious beginning, was in business.

In the 1890s, under the leadership of Irvin's son Arthur Hoyt Scott, the firm made its name as a market pioneer with the production of not only the world's first toilet rolls but also America's first paper towels. By 1913, Scott's annual sales were in excess of one million dollars.

By now Scott had brought the full weight of US industrial know-how to bear on the production process. Its 'Fourdrinier' machine produced sheets of toilet paper at a Gargantuan rate: around 152 metres of paper were squeezed out every minute. These emerged in sizes more suitable for Emperor Hongwu than for the contemporary supermarket trolley – nearly four metres across – and so they had to be chopped up into neat, shopper-friendly portions of 10 centimetres in width. There were either six hundred and fifty or a thousand sheets per portion.

Nineteen-fifteen saw Scott wrong-foot its competitors by eschewing roll-based bumfodder and returning to retro, Gayetty-style single sheets, pushing the new format with the faintly mystifying slogan 'It's the counted sheet that counts!'. The Jazz Age brought further advertising innovation, with the long-legged, top-hatted Mr Thirsty Fibre – a poster-boy for hygienic absorbency – making his debut in 1921. Another landmark was passed in 1955, when ScotTissue became the first toilet paper ever to be advertised on television.

After the firm was brought into the Kimberly-Clark fold

in 1995, the earnings of the newly-formed personal-hygiene megalith hit an unprecedented high: $1.34 billion, or £2.37 a share. The Scott wing of the firm passed the billion-dollar mark in its own right in 2006. There's money in that there bumfodder.

And the firm continues to innovate: 2010 saw the launch of Scott Tube Free – 'the first coreless bath tissue for the home'.

CHARMIN

The Hoberg Paper Company of Green Bay, Wisconsin, was the original manufacturer of Charmin toilet paper: production began in 1928. Charmin rolls were aimed squarely at the feminine end of the market and decorated with the silhouette of an elegant lady; the typeface on the powder-blue packaging was copied from the script on a lady's hatbox. They took their name from an employee's unrefined pronunciation of 'charming'; in the 1950s, Hoberg went the whole hog and changed their name to the Charmin Paper Company.

This was a bit of a waste of time, however, as in 1957 Charmin was steamrollered – that is, acquired – by Procter & Gamble. The firm founded in 1837 by candle-maker William Procter and soap-maker James Gamble was already a corporate titan, having moved from selling soap and candles to the Union army in the US Civil War to cornering the market in shampoo, toothpaste, detergent and many other products in the first half of the twentieth century.

By this time, the elegant Charmin woman had been elbowed off the packaging by a grinning baby. The brand went from strength to strength. Apart from the 1973 patenting of a new technique for imparting additional soft-ness to the paper, innovation seems to have been largely confined to the inclusion of more and more rolls within a single package. Charmin had been one of the first brands to sell four-packs; now there was simply no stopping them. Six rolls in 1978! Twelve rolls in 1986!

Eventually, the firm decided that simply selling huge packs of rolls wasn't enough. The rolls themselves had to be huge, too! So in 2005, along came the earth-shaking MegaRoll, containing four times as many sheets as a normal roll. The only snag was that the MegaRoll was too big to fit on a standard toilet-roll holder – so it was sold in tandem with the Charmin Extender toilet-roll-holder augmenta-tion device.

In the early days, these brands and others (Jeyes, Izel, Springfield, Prince) were mostly made from esparto grass (also known, not reassuringly, as 'needle grass') and was shiny and unabsorbent. In one eye-watering advertisement from the 1930s, Northern Tissue – offering a startling insight into just how low consumers' expectations were for their mass-pro-duced bumfodder – promised that their paper was 'splinter free!'. Considering the implications of this, it's somewhat mystifying that toilet paper ever caught on at all: surely even the cold kiss of the corn-cob or mussel shell was preferable to an unexpected splinter in the anus. Only those with the most baroque personal preferences, surely, would opt for a wipebreech that couldn't be used without an ever-present risk of perineal spikage.

But none of this is to suggest that these early manufacturers weren't extremely concerned about the well-being of their customers' vulnerable underparts.

In fact, the claims made by many early manufacturers went beyond mere comfort; they essentially promised to be panacaeas for all your rear-end afflictions.

Paging Doctor Bumfodder

'That Toilet Paper as a vehicle for remedies for Hemorrhoids would be of great value is obvious,' begins the promotional blurb for a mid-1880s packet of Albany Medicated. It goes on to assert that 'as a matter of fact fully twenty per cent of 'the paper's weight is due to the remedial agents it contains'. And these aren't just any old remedial agents: no, Albany Medicated contains 'only those indorsed [sic] by the medical profession'.

In another ad, from 1886, a doctor – one FM Johnson, MD – is roped in to offer a ringing testimonial: 'Gentlemen,' he announces, addressing the Albany paper-makers, 'your Medicated Toilet Paper is useful in the treatment of Anal diseases' (the same ad warns – no doubt worryingly to those reared on the out-house almanac – that 'printed paper is a cause of Hemorrhoids').

Majestic's medicated paper made perhaps the grandest claims

AN ARMY MARCHES ON ITS BUMFODDER

The arrival of army-issue loo-roll meant that hygiene didn't have to be the first casualty of war.

Strangely, none of these piles-obsessed manufacturers and their pet medics bothered to point out the real medical value of toilet paper: its fundamental role of providing a barrier between the human hand and the teeming legions of bacteria, fungi, viruses and protozoa that dwell in the human bowel. No toilet-goer wants colonies of spore-bearing anaerobes, pseudomonads, lactobacilli and enterococci making themselves comfortable in their underpants (the toilet-goer's underpants, that is; pseudomonads don't wear underpants).

Walter T Hughes MD, a US specialist in infectious diseases, has pointed out that 'in the centuries before toilet paper, plagues of dysentery, typhoid and cholera scourged

---

the world', taking a particularly heavy toll in situations where hygiene facilities weren't up to much – such as battlefields. Hughes cites the epidemic of dysentery that struck the Persian army of Xerxes in around 480 BCE, reducing the force from 800,000 men to 400,000 and no doubt making the plains of Macedonia an unbelievably unpleasant place to be.

'One can easily appreciate the ease of fecal-oral transmission in these adverse circumstances,' Dr Hughes notes.

In more recent (but still pre-loo-roll) conflicts, typhoid was the major killer: in the US Civil War, for instance, the disease – a deeply horrible cocktail of fever, vomiting, coughing, headaches, rashes and disorientation – afflicted 80 out of a thousand soldiers every year. Infection rates were almost twice as high in the Spanish-American War of 1898.

In 1905, the loo-roll revolution finally reached the front line. A report from the US Surgeon General stressed the importance of hygiene – and noted approvingly that 'the issue of toilet paper is now authorized where posts have sewer connections'.

By the first World War, typhoid incidence was down to around three cases per 1,000 soldiers; by the second World War, it had dropped to less than 0.1 per 1,000.

Of course, correlation doesn't prove causation; toilet paper was only one element of a wider trend in the direction of better hygiene and improved sanitation. But it was still worth getting excited about – especially if you were trying to sell the stuff.

of all – not only for its own efficacy, but for toilet paper – 'the greatest boon the art of paper making has developed' – as a whole. 'The consumption of [Toilet] Paper,' the packaging declares, 'is the measure of a nation's culture.'

The advertisers of Eagle Tissue – produced not on a roll but in the far more prestigious form of a booklet – take a line that suggests they're selling a gourmet foodstuff rather than a wad of wipebreech. Eagle 'is made from the highest grade of unbleached pulp and twice refined Manila, beaten in sparkling mountain water,' they assert. 'It contains no foreign matter of any description.' What's more, 'even an excessive quantity will not clog nor obstruct the plumbing'.

They go on to stake a claim for Eagle's Vermont tissue mills as 'the oldest plant in the U.S. for the manufacture of high grade toilet tissue'. The plant apparently 'enjoys a climatic condition admirable suited to the production of fine tissue'. Worried about immigrant workers inserting foreign matter into your elite toilet tissue? No need! 'The majority of the workers at the Mills are descendants of the original employees: characteristic New England Craftsmen.'

And the market celebrated innovation as well as heritage. Among the most curious developments was Springfield's oval toilet roll, which seems to have had no observable benefits other than its daringly non-circular shape.

The names of many of the papers marketed in these early days suggest that toilet rolls had an air of romance that has since, sadly, somehow been lost: 'Nile Queen', 'Beau Monde' and 'Moon-light', for instance, would all make equally suitable names for luxury yachts (although the mysterious glamour of 'Nile Queen' is undermined by the packaging's frank assurance that 'it contains no harsh, gritty substance': 'This is a safe tissue! We invite you to ask your physician for his opinion').

A Scott ad from the 1920s perfectly captured the mood of delicate if slightly desperate aspiration. Beneath an illustration of two fashionable cloche-hatted ladies, the text reads: 'Women sense it immediately – the atmosphere of elegance and refinement – those necessary little appointments, noticed but not discussed.' Then it bumps up the class-consciousness: 'ScotTissue has made a place for itself in well-conducted homes. It is the choice of discriminating women everywhere ... Peculiarly adapted to the needs of women of intuitive daintiness.'

Manufacturers also sought to strike an exotic note by giving their toilet papers names designed to evoke the mysterious Orient. However, geopolitics soon intervened: 'Mikado', 'San Toi' and 'Japanese Tar' in the UK and 'Japacrik' and 'Anzora' in the US didn't last long after the Japanese air force bombed Pearl Harbor in 1941.

There were, though, more manly, rugged options. While 'Lucky Dutchman' traded on its roguishness, 'Life Guard' took as its public face the grimacing, whiskered visage of a weather-beaten old sea-dog.

Another grimacing visage appeared in a notorious ad for Scott in 1931. 'I've got to have a ... minor operation,' mutters a frowning businessman in a Scott magazine advert. 'More serious than most men realize,' the ad warns, 'the troubles caused by harsh toilet tissue.'

The ad had a number of distaff equivalents. In one, from 1930, a deathly-looking woman lies limply on her bed, illustrating the empowering slogan: 'Woman are more susceptible, doctors say ... to troubles caused by harsh toilet tissue.'

The following copy was, following the trademark Scott Company house style, arresting and frightening in equal parts. 'There is no form of human illness quite so humiliating as rectal trouble,' it began. 'Yet in millions of homes women are exposing themselves and their families daily to ailments of this nature.'

A caption gravely adds: 'At least 15 painful diseases can be caused or aggravated by improper tissue, warns a prominent New York hospital specialist.'

But these ads were soft stuff indeed compared to the Scott Company's masterpiece: the 'black glove' of 1931, the bleak pinnacle of Scott's early 30s campaign and surely one of the most terrifying advertisements ever to find a place in the *Ladies' Home Journal*.

The image is stark: a clinically white sheet, an array of gleaming surgical instruments, and a hand, clad in a glove of thick black rubber. 'Often the only relief from toilet tissue illness,' the slogan reads (managing to suggest that 'toilet tissue illness' is a recognised medical condition). Consumers who managed to get past the photo and slogan without dropping everything and running for the high hills were then subjected to another lecture from the haemorrhoid-fixated Scott ad-men. It's the usual litany: 'Astonishing percentage of rectal cases ... traceable to inferior toilet paper ... protect your family's health ... eliminate a needless risk.' The words are so much prattle – but the image of the black rubber glove lingers in the mind.

Following criticism from the American Medical Association, Scott eventually back-tracked on its doom-laden claims – but pledged to undertake trials in order to prove beyond dispute that 'improperly made toilet tissue is a menace to health'.

Madison Avenue was by no means done. In Depression-era America, with luxury somewhat out of fashion, advertisers increasingly realised that the easiest way to the cash-strapped shopper's pocket was through her children. Unerringly, they picked out a weak spot, and hammered at it mercilessly: this was the golden age of guilt-based advertising.

Everything from Cocomalt ('Whose fault when children are

frail?') to pencils to cereal to Postum coffee substitute ('Held back by Coffee . . . this boy never had a fair chance') was pushed by the ad-men riffing on maternal anxiety and the dread of being – or (just as importantly) being seen to be – a bad parent. Scott's toilet paper ('Soft as Old Linen') latched on to the trend to great effect. In one iconic ad, a little girl sits unhappily at her school desk. 'Mary was so fidgety she couldn't concentrate,' the headline reads. 'I was shocked to find that harsh toilet tissue was the cause.'

'When I asked Mary what was the matter, she complained of an itching,' the text continues, ominously. A friend at Mother's Club suggests that the problem is 'harsh or impure' toilet tissue, and recommends Scott's – and lo, the problem is resolved. Here the advertiser butts in: 'Cases like this are common,' he warns – and that fact that it *is* a 'he' is made pretty clear when he adds: 'Women and girls especially, because of their peculiar requirements, need a soft, highly absorbent tissue.'

Those women and their peculiar requirements. Anyway, the message was clear: buy our toilet-roll, or jeopardise your child's education.

Bumfodder For The Soul

As the 20th century dragged on, the pressures of life – particularly in war-stricken Britain – generated an increasing market for softness and comfort. We didn't want hectoring, and we didn't want astringent patent medicines applied to our sensitive underparts; we wanted babying.

The trend was led in the US by the Hoberg Paper Company, who began experimenting with soft-focus, feminine, cuddly brands as early as 1929. Charmin – advertised with an image of an elegant young woman – was the first of these, and it was hugely successful. From the 1950s, the Charmin slogan put it simply: 'It babies your skin.' Among the many advantages of this approach was that it meant no-one had to mention the ghastly purpose for which these products were intended.

Softex was one of the leading post-war brands in the UK. Its advertising still relied partly on an appeal to medical authority, but the key figure in Softex's ads of the 1950s was not a bushy-eyebrowed doctor, complete with watch-chain, medical bag and forbidding expression, but a doe-eyed, smiling young nurse – the sort that might not only tend to our poor, powdered-egg-ravaged bottoms, if required, but also tuck us in, tell us everything will be all right, and give us a night-night kiss upon the brow.

Andrex – whose pioneering two-ply paper had been manufactured since the 1940s at the St Andrew's mill in Walthamstow, north-east London – went one better, going all-out for the babification market with an image of a gurgling infant. 'For babies, for mothers, for folk with tender skin – for EVERYONE', read the slogan. Andrex toilet tissue was 'cotton-wool soft'. In 1957, Andrex launched the first pink toilet paper. It was all enough to make the 'Life Guard' sea-dog choke on his Fisherman's Friend – but Andrex had set a template for mainstream toilet-roll marketing for the rest of the century.

Bronco, meanwhile, continued to plough a parallel own no-frills furrow, targeting financially straitened post-war consumers with promises not of comfort but of economy: 'How many sheets are you getting?' the ads demanded. 'Insist on knowing what you get for your money!'

Scott, in the US, offered a strikingly sexist take on the same theme. An ad in *Life* magazine in the early 60s featured a picture of a woman carrying a bag of groceries, and beneath it the legend: 'The Original Computer'.

Somewhere in that head [the ad goes on], among the bobby-pins, the hair-do, the perfume and the problems, there is a thing that makes calculations and decisions. This tricky little thinking center is the oldest instrument of progress in the human race … This feminine computer is concerned with one thing above all others: VALUE.

Beginning with the charming premise that 'a woman in a store is a mechanism, a prowling computer', the ad goes on to outline Scott's basic premise: 'If we offer our products to the homemaker at a fair price, and of uncompromising quality, she will recognise their honest value and buy them.'

In the US of the late nineteen-seventies, this kind of approach was taken up by a majority of manufacturers. Pulp prices had rocketed, and the industry's electricity bills – already high thanks to the labour-intensive process of blow-drying wet wood-pulp – had been hiked as a result of the oil crisis (itself a consequence of an embargo imposed by the Arab nations of OPEC in response to US policy on Israel).

'Manufacturers passed along the increases until consumers finally balked,' industry analyst Jack Saltzman noted. 'Suddenly price had become more important than softness.'

The manufacturers' response was to push out more budget-priced rolls, masking the compromises they were forced to make through barely noticeable adjustments in length, width and thickness. In September 1982, *New York* magazine published an article exposing these shortcuts. Rolls of the 'Marca' and 'Banner' brands, journalist Bernice Kanner revealed, had been trimmed from the standard size of 4.5 inches × 4.4 inches to 4.5 inches by 4.125 inches; 'White Cloud' now contained only 300 sheets per roll, down from 375 at the turn of the decade and 500 in 1977.

PUPPY LOVE

So your symbol of cleanliness and hygiene is a *dog*? It'll never catch on.

In the UK, toilet-paper advertising was no longer designed either to make you consider your anal diseases or worry about your bank balance. It was just there to make you go 'Aahhhh'. Cue the Andrex puppy.

Andrex was the first loo-roll firm to earn permission to advertise its product on British TV. Their cute golden labrador pup – the brainchild of ad-man Raymond Dinkin – first appeared in an Andrex ad in 1972, capering about and making a mess of people's loo-rolls. A dog might seem like a strange choice of mascot for a product promoting personal hygiene – something which dogs, for all their undoubted qualities, are seldom associated with – but the puppy clearly had enduring star quality: more than 130 puppy-based Andrex ads were to follow. From 1999, they were the work of advertisers J Walter Thomson – the same firm, interestingly, that cooked up the Scott 'black glove' campaign back in the 30s.

In 2002, with their puppy hitting 30 (133 in dog years ...), Andrex hosted a series of celebratory parties at children's hospitals across the UK. A marketing man – showing little consideration for the nation's collective gag-reflex – explained that 'we all have an emotional attachment to the Andrex puppy', which 'embodies positive qualities such as kindness and trust' – central, of course, to the deliberations of any toilet-paper purchaser. In 2004, the puppy became the first-ever brand icon to be recreated in wax at Madame Tussaud's in London.

But the happy days couldn't last. In 2010, the Andrex puppy was tied in a burlap bag with a brick and thrown into a canal – figuratively speaking, of course. Andrex 'refreshed the brand'; a CGI puppy – apparently modelled on 'the movements, mannerisms and personalities' of thousands of puppies studied by animators – was brought in. The flesh-and-blood Andrex puppy was no more.

It may have been for the best. The dopey puppy wouldn't have been suited to the more hard-edged era of loo-roll advertising that the turn of the twenty-teens ushered in.

In October 2009, the *New York Times* reported on an emerging trend among bumfodder manufacturers. The central theme was the rise of the flushable moistened tissue or 'wet-wipe' as an adjunct to the main loo-roll market (only 1 per cent of wet-wipe users, it seems, use wet-wipes alone for post-toilet cleansing: they are not a replacement for toilet paper, but only an additional step in the cleansing process). While the emergence of the wet-wipe is, of course, very interesting in its own right, the *real* hook in the story is the strategies that the big firms are adopting in order to sell these new variations.

Cottonelle, Andrex's US cousin, ran one ad that featured – alongside the still-extant Cottonelle puppy – the slogan: 'The gentle care you give to your face, hands and legs, also goes to your tush.'

The product was no longer about strength and softness, the advertisers told the *Times*; the Cottonelle brand was now a 'personal care brand', which is – of course – 'a much more emotional space'.

Rival bumfers Charmin, meanwhile, took to selling their rolls with depictions of bears with streamers of loo-roll still adhering to their hind-parts. Taking the whole thing into the internet age, the firm also posted a video online in which an actor, alarmingly, provides a 'product demo'. Thankfully, this involves only smeared toothpaste.

'It is the most clearly that we have laid it out so far,' said brand manager Jack Rubin. Mark that 'so far'.

Still, it's probably some time before any mainstream bumfodder-company comes up with anything to match the admirable candour of visual artist Jed Ela. In 1999, Ela set out to challenge preconceived ideas about marketing and bottom-wiping. He manufactured and sold a brightly-packaged, commercial-looking 2-ply toilet-roll, promising 'pillow softness' and made from 100 per cent recycled paper. It was called 'ShitBegone'.

7. Cabinet of Curiosities

Author's written up hideous creation, paper not for reading! (6,4)

Crossword clue by Paul in the Guardian, *October 2011*

Bureaucrats and paper go together like sculptors and marble, miners and coal, milkmen and milk – so it's surprising how often the logistics of bumfodder have caused a kerfuffle among the paper-pushers.

In 1963, Sir John Pilcher GCMG, a portly and jovial British diplomat, was examined by Harley Street doctor John Hunt, who determined that Pilcher was suffering from haemorrhoids. Hunt subsequently wrote to his friend Dr Cornelius Medvei, the principal medical officer in charge at the Foreign and Commonwealth Office, to say: '[My patient] thinks that the government lavatory paper is out of date and extremely bad for his complaint and he has asked me if there is any chance of it being changed to a softer type.'

Obligingly, Medvei looked into the matter. His findings were predictable: it was a matter of cost. The hard, shiny, 'out of date' paper issued by the Government was simply the most cost-effective way of keeping the bottoms of the British civil service in good order. Cost mattered; it was the taxpayer, after all, who was footing the bill.

Medvei explained that if toilet-roll costs increased even by as little as 'half a farthing daily', it would cost the government an extra £130,000 a year.

Files disclosed in 2005 to mark the first anniversary of the Freedom of Information Act paint an amusing picture of the 18-year Bumfodder Wars that followed.

A groundswell of pro-soft-paper sentiment began to make itself felt in the corridors of Whitehall. One member of the Treasury's typing pool wrote to Medvei, urging him to help 'us poor females' to avoid 'damage to our delicate parts'.

But a medical report of 1967 threatened to turn the tide, warning that soft paper was 'distinctly more pervious to infections such as dysentery'; in 1970, Prof Sir Gordon Wilson at the School of Hygiene and Tropical Medicine stated decisively – and to the Government's satisfaction – that hard, shiny paper was healthier.

An HM Stationery Office accountant reiterated the financial case in 1971: 'If we switched to soft tissue for Government purchases,' he noted, 'our annual expenditure on this item would shoot up from about £170,000 to between £500,000 and £835,000.'

The anti-soft-paper resistance was being led by 'Tommy' Thomson, the chief medical adviser to the Civil Service. 'The prevailing philosophy is that we each stand on our own feet,' Thomson declared. 'So I take it that the adjunct to that is that we each sit on our own bottoms – and don't expect the state to mollycoddle them!'

One Dr Ian Taylor, meanwhile, was leading the pro-mollycoddling faction. 'The nub of the matter is that the soft paper gives a clean wipe,' he argued.

The extraordinary dispute continued throughout the 1970s. As hard paper became less widely available, the cost advantage dwindled, and the reformists' case grew stronger. In June 1980, a report from the epidemiological research laboratory finally put a lid on the matter. It was official: soft paper was healthier. Hard paper was simply too slippery to be used hygienically.

'I think HMSO and other providers should now be encouraged to supply the soft tissue variety of toilet paper,' concluded Dr Mair Thomas.

Sir John Pilcher, the piles-plagued diplomat whose sensitive rear-end caused all the fuss in the first place, is described in his entry in the Oxford Dictionary of National Biography as having 'a fund of stories, many with a Rabelaisian twist' – including, no doubt, the saga of the civil service's loo-rolls.

But to assume that this lengthy row was the most preposterous example of tortuous bumfodder logistics in the British civil service would be to grossly underestimate the resources and talents of that esteemed institution.

In 1982, the Earl of Halsbury delivered to the House of Lords an even more extraordinary instance of what he referred to as 'egg-bound bureaucracy'. The story concerned a hospital that maintained two residential hostels for its nursing staff.

'One was built approximately in the period of the Boer War, the other was built after World War II, and so the architecture and styling of each was quite different,' Halsbury explained. 'Because of that, it was felt appropriate that the toilet paper issued to the nurses in the two hostels should be different, and that one should represent the toilet paper of the Boer War and the other the modern, tissue toilet paper.

'Nobody could accept the fact that you were dealing with nurses with a common training and with a common pay scale. Death is said to level all men, and you would think that the loo did the same – but not a bit of it.'

The officials responsible for this baroque piece of administration could perhaps argue in response that the nurses should think themselves fortunate not to inhabit a hostel dating from Roman times – cold *xylospongions* and all.

COMMANDER COE'S CRISIS

War is hell. Especially when you're 200 m below the sea and all out of bumfodder.

Egg-bound bureaucracy is not the sole preserve of British administrators; in 1942, the submariners of the

USS *Skipjack* found to their frustration that American bureaucrats could be just as obtuse, and could keep just as keen an eye on the departmental toilet-roll dispenser.

In July 1941, the *Skipjack* had submitted a request for 150 rolls of toilet paper. By the following April, the rolls had still not arrived; in July, the unfulfilled request was returned to the *Skipjack*, stamped with the words 'cancelled – cannot identify'. The reply promptly despatched to the Navy Yard's supply officer by Lt. Commander James W. Coe, the *Skipjack*'s commanding officer, is worth repeating here in full (courtesy of the indispensable *Letters Of Note* website: www.lettersofnote.com):

U.S.S. SKIPJACK

84/18/S36–1
11 June, 1943

From: The Commanding Officer.
To: Supply Officer, Navy Yard, Mare Island, California.
Via: Commander Submarines, Southwest Pacific.

Subject: Toilet Paper.

Reference: (a) (6048) USS HOLLAND (5184) USS SKIP-JACK Reqn. 70–42 of July 30, 1941; (b) SO NYMI cancelled invoice No. 272836.

Enclosure: (A) Copy of cancelled invoice; (B) Sample of material requested.

1. This vessel submitted a requisition for 150 rolls of toilet paper on July 30, 1941, to USS HOLLAND. The material was ordered by HOLLAND from Supply Officer, Navy Yard, Mare Island, for delivery to USS SKIPJACK.

2. The Supply Officer, Navy Yard, Mare Island, on November 26, 1941, cancelled Mare Island Invoice No. 272836 with the stamped notation "cancelled – cannot identify". This cancelled invoice was received by SKIP-JACK on June 19, 1942.

3. During the 11–1/2 months elapsing from the time of ordering the toilet paper and the present date the SKIP-JACK personnel, despite their best efforts to await delivery of subject material have been unable to wait on numerous occasions, and the situation is now quite acute, especially during depth charge attacks by the "back-stabbers".

4. Enclosure (B) is a sample of the desired material provided for the information of the Supply Officer, Navy Yard, Mare Island. The Commanding Officer, USS SKIPJACK cannot help but wonder what is being used by Mare Island in place of this unidentifiable material, one well known to this command.

5. SKIPJACK personnel during this period has become accustomed to the use of "Ersatz" the vast amount of incoming non-essential paper work, and in so doing felt that the wish of the Bureau of Ships for "reduction of paper work" is being complied with thus effectually "killing two birds with one stone".

6. It is believed by this Command that the stamped notation "cannot identify" was possibly an error, and this is simply a case of shortage of strategic war material, the SKIPJACK probably being low on the priority list.

7. In order to cooperate in war effort at small local sacrifice, the SKIPJACK desires no further action to be taken until the end of current war which has created a situation aptly described as "War is Hell".

J.W. COE

Lt. Commander Coe's uncomfortable position later inspired a scene in the 1959 Cary Grant-Tony Curtis vehicle *Operation Petticoat*; Grant played the Coe character, Rear Admiral Matt Sherman.

But in real life, the story had a fantastical ending: when the *Skipjack* next returned to land, it was greeted at the dockside by towering pyramids of toilet rolls, fluttering toilet roll streamers, and even a brass band sporting toilet-paper neckties. This was the kind of devoted service that in 1944 earned Kimberly-Clark a US 'E' award for excellence in commercial services – for their unstinting provision of loo-roll to soldiers on the front line.

(The *Skipjack*'s welcome-home party wouldn't be the last time a military installation would be bedecked with bumfodder: during the Gulf War, US troops in Saudi Arabia used toilet paper to help camouflage their tanks.)

Leaving aside the determined perversity of civil servants worldwide, it's fairly clear that the western world has made a lasting accommodation with toilet paper. The loo-roll, for the time being at least, is a fixture of our society. Two stories from the 1970s stand out as high-water marks of America's love affair with the product they know simply as 'TP'.

In 1973, Wisconsin congressman Howard Froehlich voiced concerns about the possibility of a national shortage of toilet paper; that night, talk-show host Johnny Carson riffed on the theme in his opening monologue. Viewers didn't find it funny. Instead, they dashed out in their hundreds to their nearest convenience stores, and panic-bought TP by the trolley-load.

Five years later, *TV Guide* magazine conducted a poll to identify the most famous man in America. Ex-president Richard Nixon came first; evangelist Billy Graham came second; and in third was Mr Whipple, the genial – if fictional – grocer who since 1964 had advertised Charmin toilet paper (in a typical ad, Mr Whipple would reprimand a female customer with his catchphrase, 'Please don't squeeze the Charmin!' – only to be seen, moments later, hypocritically squeezing the irresistibly soft rolls himself. Mr Whipple was named after a PR man at one of Procter & Gamble's ad agencies and played by the actor Dick Wilson, who was rewarded for his efforts with a lifetime supply of Charmin).

The eco-impact of our collective loo-roll habit is an issue that many environmentalists rank alongside such higher-profile problems as gas-guzzling cars and unsustainable fast-food diets. As with these other problems, it's the US that attracts the greatest opprobrium. In addition to their high levels of consumption, Americans are likely to use high-impact, lotion-infused, multi-ply papers made from virgin timber (whereas in Europe and South America, up to 40 per cent of toilet paper comes from recycled products).

'This is a product that we use for less than three seconds and the ecological consequences of manufacturing it from trees is enormous,' Allen Hershkowitz, a senior scientist at the Natural Resources Defence Council, commented in February 2009. 'Future generations are going to look at the way we make toilet paper as one of the greatest excesses of our age.'

It's not only the manufacture of toilet paper that has environmentalists puckering their brows in concern; its disposal can also be a minefield.

One of the foremost dilemmas for the modern bumfodder-merchant is the question of striking a balance between, on the one hand, a paper that is flimsy enough to dissolve harmlessly in the sewers, and, on the other, a paper that is so flimsy that it doesn't wait until its work is done before falling to pieces – with distasteful consequences.

It was this latter worry that led to Charmin launching a hyper-strong paper for the British market in 2000. The industry's market research experts had obviously excelled themselves: startlingly detailed statistics indicated that the worldwide wiping public was split on the question of whether to wad the paper into a bunch before wiping, or to fold it carefully into a manageable square. Around 40 per cent were found to wad, and 40 per cent to fold (a puzzling 20 per cent reported that they preferred to 'wrap', an avant garde tactic that presumably involves winding the roll of paper around the wiping hand).

Men were apparently more likely to fold; women generally preferred to wad. Crucially, there was also a split down the Atlantic divide: US wipers are more likely than those in the UK to scrunch. Britain, *contra* Napoleon, is a nation of bum-fodder-folders.

Because folded tissue is less robust when wet than its scrunched equivalent, Charmin produced a brand with 'transient wet strength', designed to prevent 'premature disintegration'. Protests from rival wipebreech giant Kimberly-Clark, claiming that this new breed of superbumf would play merry hell with sewage-plant filters, forced Charmin to scale back the paper's 'transient strength' by half – and prompted the Association of Makers of Soft Tissue Papers to draft a voluntary testing protocol for 'flushability' and 'dispersability'.

This was by no means a new concern for the industry. Indeed, the tag-line in one of the very first Albany ads urged consumers to consider not only the treatment of their piles but also the condition of their pipes: 'PHYSICIANS' AND PLUMBERS' BILLS AVOIDED BY USING PERFORATED PAPER ... CLOGGED PIPES WITH CONSEQUENT IMPURE AIR AND DISEASE PREVENTED.'

Econauts might want to bear in mind that, when it comes to saving paper, technique counts for a great deal. To fold, or to wad? Dave Praeger weighs up the alternatives:

> While wadding creates a thicker buffer, folding gives more grasping surface. A wadder thus requires more paper than a folder to achieve the same wiping surface area, assuming the folder creates a suitably thick parcel. Thus a wadder requires more paper than a folder, and can expect higher lifetime toilet paper expenditure. Then again, the extra seconds per poop it takes to fold the paper add up as well.

This isn't the only big decision the modern wiper has to make. In the first instance is the question (widely debated at one time in the letters pages of certain women's magazines) of whether to have the toilet roll oriented 'overhand' on its holder – that is, with the end facing away from the wall – or 'underhand'. Then there is the number of sheets used per procedure; whether to sit, crouch or stand; whether to reach around the back, or go through the front way; whether to wipe back-to-front, or front-to-back; whether, in the end, the job is complete, or whether a last safety-wipe is required ...

You probably haven't thought much about these questions before. In fact, it may not have occurred to you that other people might not do these things the way you do them. And you're probably now thinking: *other people are* weird.

They are, in fact, weirder than you might have supposed.

Bumfoddballs

For instance, there are those who take the whole 'folding' business even further – further, you might think, than sanity should permit. Loo-roll origami, anyone?

In fact, it's not just origami, but also loo-roll papercraft, sewing and kanzashi, that are covered in Linda Wright's 2010 *Toilet Paper Crafts for Holidays and Special Occasions*. 'Take toilet paper to a new dimension, and revolutionize your use of a bathroom basic!' the book urges. 'This collection of 60 stylish projects will add a joyous touch and festive flair to any holiday or special occasion – including birthdays, weddings, and Christmas.'

Some have taken toilet-paper art even further than that. Visiting the aeroplane lavatory while on a flight in 2010, artist Nina Katchadourian 'spontaneously put a tissue paper toilet cover seat cover over my head and took a picture in the mirror

BRAIN-BENDING BUMFODDER

You might think that the manufacture of 'Angel So Soft' – to take an example at random from *Toilet Paper Crafts* – is as advanced as toilet-paper folding can get. You'd be wrong.

In 2005, US high-school student Britney Gallivan took on a new project to earn extra credit in her mathematics class. Her challenge was to dispel the commonly-held belief that it is impossible to fold a piece of paper in half more than seven times. She set to work on a length of toilet paper – and ended up folding it in half fifteen times.

You're probably wondering what the limiting equation is for single direction toilet-paper folding, where L is the minimum possible length of the material, t is material thickness, and n is the number of folds possible in one direction. It's quite simple:

$$L = \frac{nt}{6} \, (2^n + 4) \, (2^n - 1)$$

In 2012, a team of maths students at St Mark's School in Southborough, Massachussetts, broke Britney's record – they folded a piece of toilet paper in half 13 times. The 'piece' of paper was 16km long. The resultant wad was 76cm high, and comprised 8,192 layers of toilet paper.

using my cellphone. The image evoked 15th-century Flemish portraiture.'

Naturally enough, Katchadourian, inspired, went on to create more than 2,500 pictures and videos on some 70 different flights. She has fashioned headwear from toilet seat covers, toilet paper, seat-cushions and other paraphernalia to create self-portraits in the style of such masters as Robert Campin and Rogier van der Weyden. As one does.

There's obviously something about the humble loo-roll that prompts people to attempt bizarrely arcane feats. In March 2011, for example, David Unfried of Fulton, Missouri, set the record for stacking ten toilet rolls one on top of another. He did it in 5.8 seconds. *Why* he did it is another question altogether.

Another odd feat took place in 1995, when Philadelphia city employee Ricardo Jefferson was accused of stealing $34,000 worth of toilet paper from the stadium of the Philadelphia Eagles – surely history's greatest bumfodder-theft. The true scale of the heist may never be known: 'We don't really know how long this was going on,' said city spokesman Tony Radwanski. 'We only looked at a ten-month period from October 1994 to August 1995.'

Jefferson could have been running his scam – ordering twice as much paper as was necessary, and selling on the rest (Philadelphia presumably supporting a buoyant TP black market) – for years. That no-one has yet made a Hollywood movie out of the story is simply astounding. Showing symptoms of the sort of pun-fever that all too often infects local news coverage, Tony Radwanski added: 'Man, he really wiped that stadium clean.'

In 2011, the British tabloid *The Sun* newspaper broke the story of another alleged loo-roll theft. This was not on the scale of Jefferson's heist, but its supposed victim was even more worshipful than an NFL football team. Eagles fans might be renowned throughout the US for their loyalty and fervour, but they're nothing compared to the world's 1.15 billion Catholics – each of whom, presumably, was shocked and outraged to read in the *Sun* that the pop singer Myleene Klass had stolen the Pope's loo roll.

Klass claimed to have nabbed the Papal bumfodder while filming on location at the Pope's summer residence in Castel Gandolfo, Italy.

'The Pope wasn't actually there, but I did take some loo roll,' she confided to the *Sun*. 'And I made Christmas presents out of it. I stuck a piece of tissue, and I'd write, "Papal loo roll; a tissue. Bless you." It's so bad it's good, right?'

She went on to describe the holy roll as 'very special because it's got papal wreaths embossed all over it in little green laurel leaves'.

Sounds tasteful, low-key and all-in-all very much in keeping with the best interior-decorating traditions of the church of Rome. But some felt that the details of the story did not quite ring true – and thus began a diverting Fleet Street spat that was brought to an end only when the Vatican itself stepped in to set the record straight.

Klass's story was questioned by the *Guardian* journalist Marina Hyde, who accused the singer – in so many words – of fabricating the incident for purposes of publicity.

After being informed by a Deep Throat-style confidant that toilet paper throughout the Papal state was, in fact, not bedecked with leaves but, rather, 'uniform – plain white and a touch below Andrex standard', Hyde challenged Klass to verify her story and produce as proof the pilfered wipebreech of Benedict XVI – so that 'we can lay this important debate to rest, and get back to disporting ourselves with such fripperies as the eurozone debt crisis'.

Klass promptly published a photo of the loo roll, resplendent in a frame and marked with a laurel-leaved 'R' monogram, on her Twitter account – so Hyde turned to a higher authority. Press contacts at the Vatican (presumably always glad of a little light relief, what with One Thing and Another) confirmed, Hyde reported, 'not only that the bog roll is not Benedict's, nor some monogrammed indulgence left over from his Ratzinger years, but that it could not possibly have been obtained from any truly private quarter'.

Of course, the Pope might at times be infallible, but the same does not necessarily go for his press officers. Klass stood by her story. The mystery of the stolen Papal loo-roll went unresolved.

But it's not only pop stars and/or journalists who are liable to let sound and sober judgment fall by the wayside where toilet paper is concerned. As a society of consumers, we are all surely guilty of an enormous collective marble-loss in this regard.

Would a sane society ever have created a market for black toilet paper, as launched in 2006 by the Portuguese paper firm Renova and described by the firm's MD, Paulo Miguel Pereira da Silva, as 'neither solely a product, an object or a communication tool' but, rather, a combination of all three? If the western world had all its faculties in their proper places, would 7 per cent of respondents to an industry survey, when asked what features they considered important in a public toilet, tick the box marked 'custom-printed toilet-paper with humorous sayings for their reading pleasure'?

It seems that the modern demand for unrelenting stimulus does not stop at the toilet door.

Nowadays, there are few limits to what can be printed on a roll of toilet paper. A stylish leopard-print pattern? No problem! – *and*, if you buy it from the Designer Toilet Roll Company of West Sussex, England, it 'even comes packaged in a beautiful presentation box set to impress just everyone'! Also in the Designer Toilet Roll Company's range are papers printed with images of barbed wire, ladybirds, the words 'Happy Birthday!', and – for the romantics out there – a 'Just Married' logo.

Maybe you want a work-out for your brain while your bowel goes through the motions (or rather, *vice versa*). Then you'll be wanting one of the widely available crossword-puzzle rolls (described by one manufacturer as 'ideal for long train journeys'); each sheet carries a brain-teasing puzzle. For those more number-minded, Sudoku loo-roll is also, inevitably, available.

(Speaking of puzzles, the solution to the cryptic crossword clue with which this chapter began is, of course, *toilet roll*: the author 'written up' – i.e. written backwards – is Eliot, and the 'hideous creation' is a troll, giving TOILE + TROLL – although, as we now know, toilet roll can *sometimes* be for reading.)

Books of one sort or another have been published on toilet paper since the late 1970s, for people who (a) have a lot of time to kill and (b) think that the toilet is the nicest place in their house to curl up with a book. In addition to volumes of puzzles, the library of available loo-roll literature includes *The Book Of Lists* and *The Dieter's Guide To Weight Loss During Sex*. Fully paid-up members of the Digital Age can even order loo-rolls printed with the Twitter feed of a Tweeter of their choice.

At the other end of the busyness spectrum, those who simply haven't time to fumble for a light switch when visiting the loo outside daylight hours can buy glow-in-the-dark toilet rolls (no, they're nothing to do with the United Kingdom Atomic Energy Authority). These can, however, backfire (so to speak). A note on the side of the packaging warns: 'Glow in the dark coating can rub off the toilet roll. It is not dangerous, but please ensure you wash your hands thoroughly after use.' One might think that it would be an area of the body other than the hands that might be of more concern in this regard. No-one, surely, wants a ghostly green glow emanating from their anus – although, of course, it's never easy to be certain of such things in these permissive times.

Yet another unexpected niche in the market has been filled by the recently-established Ministry of Toilet Rolls. The people behind the Ministry used to sell rosettes to football fans; now – in a development that might say a great deal about modern football – their stall outside Tottenham Hotspur's White Hart Lane stadium in north London sells loo rolls emblazoned with the logo of Arsenal, Spurs' local rivals. Strangely, the Ministry advises 'tearing off 1 or 2 sheets and placing them inside your normal toilet paper for maximum pleasure'. This seems to cast grave doubts on the fortitude of the Ministry's paper: is it in fact a flimsy product that, with the application of even a minimal amount of pressure, comes entirely to pieces? Please feel free to insert your own Spurs joke here.

The Ministry's enterprising product range does not, of course, represent the only historical confluence of football and bumfodder. At English football matches during the 1970s and 80s, the practice of flinging toilet rolls on to the pitch was a cornerstone of what passed for terrace etiquette. Nobody knows why. But one player, in any case, seems to have found inspiration in this reckless loo-roll littering: Francis Lee, Manchester City's star striker in the late 60s, went on to make millions in retirement as a big player in the recycled toilet-paper industry.

It should perhaps be pointed out that the practice of printing on sheets of toilet roll is not entirely a modern phenomenon. It may have taken until 2010 for someone to patent 'Toilet Paper With Advertising Effect' (featuring ads in any language, or even in Braille: 'therefore, when the toilet paper is used, a user can read the content on the toilet paper, so that the advertising effect is achieved'), but the principle had been around for years.

And this was no mere hack-work: in the 1930s, one of the century's most celebrated illustrators got in on the act.

William Heath Robinson's modern reputation is built principally on his beautifully inked drawings of crackpot contraptions – the Elegant And Interesting Apparatus Designed To Overcome Once And For All The Difficulties Of Conveying Green Peas To The Mouth (1929), for instance. But he was also established as an illustrator of books – he produced a suite of pictures for *Gargantua And Pantagruel* in 1904 – and as a hugely successful commercial artist. In this latter capacity he had produced adverts for, among other things, Duroid Macadam and Mackintosh's Toffee; in 1932, he was approached by Newton Chambers, the makers of Izal Medicated Toilet Paper.

The resulting sheets each feature trademark Heath Robinson gadgetry: fortunately (or unfortunately, depending on the tastelessness of your sense of humour), the gags focus not on the bottom-wiping process – imagine what Heath Robinson might have come up with if he'd applied himself to that! – but on the various applications of Izal disinfectant.

Thus, we have An Ingenious Apparatus For Izalising A Broody Hen, Testing The New Sprinkler Izal Bottle, Time Test Of Germicidal Powers of Different Strengths of Izal, The Afterglow Of An Izal Bath, and – far less distressing than it sounds – The Latest Surgical Equipment For The Treatment Of Wounds (featuring, you'll be amazed to hear, a large vat of Izal).

Perhaps not the most inspiring subject for a man who had also illustrated the works of Shakespeare, Poe, Kipling and Cervantes, but even Heath Robinson had to pay the rent somehow.

Once You Have Them By The Bumfodder, Their Hearts And Minds Will Follow

The idea of persuasive toilet paper re-emerged in darker circumstances a few years later; this time, it was selling not Izal, but ideas – this wasn't advertising, but, rather, advertising's shadowy close cousin: propaganda.

During the first World War, Heath Robinson had in fact made a name for himself as a creator of jovial anti-German propaganda: 'Huns injecting chilblain serum into British feet', 'First Lessons In Goosestep', and so on. The work was witty and charming; it was intended, above all, to keep British spirits up.

The toilet paper propaganda of the second World War was produced with a rather different aim; it was not witty, or charming, and it had about it the unpleasant whiff of desperation.

Sir Arthur 'Bomber' Harris, the Allies' Commander in Chief of Bomber Command during the second World War, was unimpressed by the widespread policy of dropping propaganda leaflets on enemy terrritory, describing it as 'a game in which we never had the slightest faith'. 'My personal view,' he wrote, 'is that the only thing achieved was largely to supply the Continent's requirements of toilet paper for the five long years of the war.' In the early years of the war, aircraft crews engaged in dropping the leaflets were jovially known as 'bumphleteers'.

But the decidedly sinister Morale Operations (MO) branch of the Office of Strategic Services (OSS) took a different view. The director of the MO was William J Donovan, whose stated aim was to develop an Allied unit with the same talent for psychological warfare as the Nazis; the MO's job was to disseminate 'black' propaganda – that is, propaganda that seems to identify with one side in a conflict but is in fact produced by the opposing side – behind enemy lines.

Thousands of sheets of propagandist toilet paper were produced at the MO's headquarters in Rome. One such sheet bore the following message (in German):

Comrades!
Enough with all this shit! We do not fight for Germany any longer but only for Hitler and Himmler. The Nazi Party has led us down this damn street but now the bigwigs only think of saving their own skin.

They let us die in the dirt. We should hold out until the last cartridge. But we need the last cartridges to free Germany from the SS shit.

Finish!! Peace!!

Others carried mocking caricatures of Hitler or other members of the Nazi high command. Under one image of the

Führer was written 'DIESE SEITE BENUTZEN!' – 'Use this side'.

Another toilet paper design depicted a sleep-deprived German civilian; underneath, a rhyme read:

Bread without butter
Eight o'clock in bed
Arse not yet warm
Air-raid warning

Food for thought, indeed, for a war-weary civilian who hears the sound of 'Bomber' Harris's squadrons droning overhead as he sits to relieve himself.

All in all, according to the *Final Report of Production and Distribution from 15 July 1944 to 15 May 1945* of the OSS MO in Rome, 334,000 sheets of propaganda toilet paper were produced; most were distributed in northern Italy, the southern city of Brindisi, and France.

The British, of course, were not to be left out of all this high-level toilet humour. Their contribution was a set of spoofs of the 50-pfennig Auxiliary Payment Certificates issued to members of the German armed forces. On the back were printed (in German) pointed witticisms, such as: 'I am a piece of Hitler's arsewipe. Nobody accepts me because nobody can buy anything with me.'

The richly comic idea of wiping your bottom on a banknote was revived by propagandists during the Korean, Vietnam and Gulf wars. For example, one satirical mock-up of the North Vietnamese 50-dong note carried a cartoon on the reverse of a squatting Vietnamese peasant and the legend: 'The Only Use For The Paper Money Of Ho Chi Minh.'

In 1993, the US magazine *Newsweek* reported on similar 'funny money' that had surfaced in Iraq. During the conflict two years earlier, someone – probably the CIA, as the army declined to take responsibility – had issued 20-dinar notes with cartoons on the back. Some mocked the dictator Saddam Hussein; others depicted empty Iraqi grocery stores. In one, a shopkeeper unrolls a reel of Iraqi banknotes from a toilet-roll dispenser; the caption, in Arabic, reads: 'At least it has a value now!'

Given a suitably tasteless sense of humour, there's no reason why this sort of japery can't be continued into times of relative peace. In 2012, German artist Georg Buchrucker unexpectedly revived the Führer-based bumfodder *motif*. His 'Draw Your Own Shitler' toilet paper featured a caricature of Hitler – minus the trademark moustache.

Users were invited to 'draw' a moustache on the glowering face. In a fetching shade of brown.

8. A Watery End

'Be it known that I, Jacob G Van Houten of the city of Trenton, State of New Jersey, have invented a new and useful Improvement in Bidet Water-Closets, of which the following is a specification.'

US Patent No. 231462

It's natural to imagine that the wiping methodology we use in our home today is the last word on the subject, the Authorised Version, the only really *normal* way to do things. There's a nice illustration of this in the 1993 sci-fi action film *Demolition Man*, in which Sylvester Stallone plays 'John Spartan', a 1990s LA cop put into cold storage and reawoken in the year 2032. A gurning, muscle-bound fish out of water in what we're encouraged to see as an unwholesomely sanitised future 'San Angeles', Spartan keeps the 20th-century flame alive by (a) swearing and (b) stubbornly wiping his bottom on paper.

But we don't have to leap into an unconvincing 2032 co-starring Sandra Bullock to see what the future holds for undercarriage hygiene. We could instead, perhaps, peruse the latest patents in the field. Who, for example, can foresee anything other than widespread acclaim and wholesale adoption for New York inventor Howard Steinberg's pioneering bumfodder-alternative: the Anus Crevice Insert?

International patent WO2011112269 gives more detail:

The protective device cover includes a solid sheet of material with an adhesive on one side which adhesive can be used to apply the cover directly onto the portion directly around and adjacent to the anus after it has been inserted into the crevice. The cover also includes slits or holes through which evacuated material may pass through.

The cover may also be made from a 'plastic-wrap' type material that adheres to human skin when pressure is applied. In an alternate embodiment, a wiping pad is provided between two layers of the cover, which traverses the hole opening when a stab string is pulled to effect at least partial cleaning in the anus area. This almost eliminates the need for toilet paper, keeps the body clean, and avoids excessive contamination.

It's hard to read it, isn't it, without recalling Keats' 'On First Looking Into Chapman's Homer': *Then felt I like some watcher of the skies/ When a new planet swims into the ken . . .*

The same goes for Jiang Zhenguang's Automatic Washer for Faeces and Urine (patent no. CN201312772), a substitute for paper that seems to resemble a small, water-filled bicycle-pump and 'can be used for washing a defecating part'.

Or perhaps, in looking to the future, we should simply survey the needs and desires of consumers – they are the ones, after all, who will steer the market in years to come. Conveniently, one US toilet-paper firm has already done this. Respondents were quizzed on the features they would like to see in the public toilets of the future – and the results weren't exactly at the Jules Verne end of the imagination scale.

The most widely-longed-for toilet feature of the future – cited by forty-two per cent of those questioned – was 'voice-activated product dispensers'. Eighteen per cent wanted 'full-time toilet attendants to be on-call' (for what purpose? We don't know); two per cent wanted modem lines and electrical outlets for laptop computers (for what purpose? We don't know – and, what's more, we're not sure we want to).

Of course, as we've seen, the next chapter in the annals of the arsewispe is already being written by the whizkids behind the Washlet and its imitators. But it's worth remembering that Toto didn't invent the water-based wipe; they only revolutionised it. Long before the Washlet, before Toto, before Kazuchika Okura, there was Madame de Prie, and her *bidet*.

Jeanne Agnès Berthelot de Pléneuf, the Marquise de Prie, in addition to being an influential intriguer under the reign of Louis XV, earned a minor place in history as the first known user of a bidet (the word is French for a little horse). In 1710, she is recorded as having received the Marc René de Voyer, Marquis d'Argenson, while astride the device (although, as the humourist Frank Muir has pointed out, how de Voyer knew what she was astride, given the voluminous skirts of the day, is a mystery: 'She might just as well,' Muir comments, 'have been astride a unicycle').

Subsequently, bidets were manufactured to order by European nobles including the Marquise de Pompadour, the Duchess of Bedford and Madame de Talmont. Advertisements for the new technology were being circulated by the mid-1700s; in 1741, the painter François Boucher depicted a glamorous young woman going about her *toilette intime* (although the instrument in use looks more like a gravy-boat than a bidet).

But for all its continental *je ne sais quoi*, the bidet has never quite caught on in the Anglophone world. We're more likely to be provoked to embarrassed sniggers and jokes about the 'dolls' bath' than to gasps of admiration. Which is, of course, quite ridiculous of us.

Poop Culture author Dave Praeger is characteristically frank on the subject.

Given an American obsession with cleanliness that far exceeds most European standards, it's odd that we haven't embraced bidets wholeheartedly. It is inconsistent with general practice: if you got poop on your arm, you'd wash it off, not smear it off. And yet, for the butt, we're content to smear.

Praeger suggests that the bidet's Frenchified name ('sounds too much like *ballet*') is the principal bar to its widespread adoption in the US. 'Market it as a "buttsink",' he urges, 'and watch bidet sales soar.'

The acerbic US film-maker Billy Wilder certainly didn't see the point of it. Travelling in France, he was asked by his wife – who had stayed in the States – to buy a bidet for their bathroom at home. In reply, she received a telegram that read: 'UNABLE OBTAIN BIDET. SUGGEST HANDSTAND IN SHOWER.'

Bidets are used widely throughout continental Europe and South America (although, mysteriously, France – the bidet's ancestral home – has seen a dramatic decline in bidet adoption since the 1970s, and has been outstripped by Italy as Europe's bidet capital).

In most eastern cultures, washing with water is a *sine qua non* after using the toilet. Muslim *haditha* suggest taking along a beaker of water for this purpose. On the Indian subcontinent, this vessel is known as a *lota*; in the Philippines it is a *tabo*, and in Indonesia a *gayung*. Many toilets in the Middle East and beyond consist of little more than a hole in the ground and a hose or water-dish, while in Turkey, even western-style toilets are fitted with a *bidet*-style nozzle. In 1961, Rotherham's Labour MP Jack Jones moaned that there were in Africa 'hundreds of thousands who do not yet know how to use toilet paper, such is the society in which we live in the world in 1961'. To which the obvious riposte is that, just possibly, those hundreds of thousands didn't *need* to know how to use toilet paper.

This, perhaps, just as well. In 1987, the slightly confused-sounding Lord John-Mackie delivered the following frightening forecast to the House of Lords. His theme was trees: do we need them?

The counter-argument is that people will not read newspapers in the future but will rely on the radio and television. People in business will not read newspapers. They will use computers, all of which will save paper.

I found it difficult to come up with an answer to that until I attended a lecture by [environmental broadcaster] Dr David Bellamy concerning the spread of civilisation and its effect on the environment. Dr. Bellamy produced the slightly indelicate statistic that if, following this civilisation, which has spread everywhere, everybody used toilet paper, there would not be a tree left. I do not know whether that is a good argument to use, but we cannot possibly say that trees will not be needed in the future.

There's a new argument for you, environmentalists: save trees, or else in future we won't have anything to wipe our bums on.

An episode in Salman Rushdie's classic 1981 novel *Midnight's Children* illuminates the understandable distaste of many non-Europeans for the western approach to personal hygiene.

The scene is India, on the brink of independence in 1947. William Methwold, the departing English estate owner, agrees to sell his property to an Indian family, on the condition that they retain the estate's entire contents – not even a lampshade is to be changed (and Methwold requests that the estate's new owners also keep up the tradition of cocktails on the lawn every day at six). The proviso does not go down well with the matriarch of the Indian family.

'For two months we must live like those Britishers?' she wails. 'You've looked in the bathrooms? No water near the pot. I never believed, but it's true, my God, they wipe their bottoms with paper only!'

9. Going Without

'Now, I prithee, go on in this torcheculative, or wipe-bummatory discourse.'

Gargantua & Pantagruel, Book I

It's not just the advent of the Washlet that suggests that the Golden Age of toilet paper – which has so far spanned more than a century and a half, from Mr Gayetty's 1857 breakthrough to the latest SuperSoft, MultiPly, UltraThick corporate contrivances – could be coming, appropriately enough, to an end.

Another factor is the environmental impact. Using ex-trees to wipe away our excrement before flushing them into the sewer just doesn't seem sustainable any more. Switching to recycled paper would help, of course: according to figures from the US Environmental Protection Agency, 470,000 trees, 1.2 million cubic feet of landfill space and 169 million gallons of water could be saved if everyone in the US traded one roll of regular toilet paper for a recycled roll.

But at present, none of America's top-selling bumfsters makes use of recycled pulp. Toilet paper accounts for 5 per cent of the US's forest products (newspapers, by way of comparison, account for 3 per cent). The market demands softness, and the softer a roll is, the more likely it is to have come from old-growth and virgin trees. This is because old trees provide longer fibres, and longer fibres make for a softer and more flexible paper; papers made from old newspapers, on the other hand, have shorter fibres, and are correspondingly rougher.

Quilted Northern Ultra Plush – the luxurious paper described by the *Washington Post* as 'the first big brand to go three-ply and three-adjective' – sold 24 million packs in 2009, bringing in more than $144 million. Money on that scale talks; in this case, what it says is 'no' to recycled loo-roll. As the *Post* says, in the US, 'soft is to toilet paper what fat is to bacon'.

Not everyone, of course, has gone happily along with the tree-intensive trend. As far back as the 1950s, while the likes of Kimberly-Clark and the Scott Company were expanding into the global bum-wiping conglomerates we know today, a New Jersey paper company was already having second thoughts about the consumption of virgin wood for such a menial purpose.

Marcal claims to have been 'committed to saving trees for two decades before Greenpeace bought its first boat'. It makes much of its toilet-paper from paper waste deposited in recycling bins in the high-rise offices of downtown Manhattan. Wipe with Marcal, and you could be having a close encounter with what was once Donald Trump's bank statement.

In Marcal's latest brands of ever-so-slightly scratchy recycled paper, we can see a penitent's hair-shirt: in 2006, the firm was pushed into bankruptcy by a $945 million lawsuit from the Environmental Protection Agency for polluting a stretch of New Jersey's Passaic River.

Of course, the bigger firms have started to make small steps towards more environmentally sound practice. Recycling still seems to be beyond the pale, but Kimberly-Clark, for instance, was recently badgered by Greenpeace into signing an agreement that will at least reduce the firm's use of ancient woodlands such as Canada's Boreal Forest to make TP. But – as numerous outraged green activists pointed out when Greenpeace declared a triumphant end to its 'Kleercut' campaign in 2009 – the deal is hardly a comprehensive victory for sustainability. Forests that date back to the last Ice Age will still be cleared in pursuit of eversofter wipebreeches; trees that might have stood since before Joseph Gayetty was born will still be cut down, pulped, folded (or wadded, according to taste), wiped with excrement, and flushed down the toilet.

In Britain, meanwhile, the supermarket chain Sainsbury's recently took the dramatic step of slimming down not its paper but, rather, the cardboard roll around which the paper is wound. The firm's rolls were shrunk from 123mm to 112mm in diameter in an attempt to save some 50 depot-to-store lorry journeys.

The Sainsbury's spokesman who stepped forward to announce the move demonstrated an all-too-rare grasp of bumfodder history.

'Perhaps it's hard to believe that centuries ago we used leaves and wool and that two-ply was only introduced in the 1960s.' he said. 'This is another step in its development, giving an essential household product a lower carbon footprint.'

BUMFLESS IN NEW YORK

No Impact Man and The Year Without Toilet Paper.

Will the people of the western world ever really lay down their Charmins, surrender their Andrexes, say byebye to their three-ply?

One man, at least, had a go: New York writer Colin Beavan, better known as No Impact Man. Beavan – and his wife and baby daughter – launched a brave experiment in the winter of 2006. They would live, as best they could, without making any impact on their environment. That meant not using carbon-fuelled transport, not throwing anything away (except things that could be composted), eating only local food – and going without toilet paper.

It was this last sacrifice that caught the media's attention. No car, sure. No imported wine, oil or tomatoes – hell, why not? But wait – *no TP?*

The *New York Times* headlined its profile of the family 'The Year Without Toilet Paper'. Aghast *Times* journalist Penelope Green reported that '*nothing* is a substitute for toilet paper, by the way; think of bowls of water and lots of air drying'.

Green rather sniffily compared the No Impact project to a Manhattanised version of the writer Henry David Thoreau's famous Walden Pond project of 1845. Thoreau spent two years in a hut he had built himself at Walden, a pleasant spot near the New England town of Concord, and did his best to live self-sufficiently: he spent much of his time reading, writing and 'sauntering', and in 1854 published *Walden*, his now-classic account of his experiences (Thoreau wrote seven drafts of the book before finally submitting it for publication: it sounds like a decidedly unsustainable use of pencil-lead, but then Thoreau had spent years apprenticed to his father as a pencil-maker, so maybe he felt he'd put enough back to justify the consumption).

Sadly, Thoreau never specifies in *Walden* what he used for bumfodder. In those pre-Gayetty days, it's likely that decamping to the countryside had little effect on Thoreau's choice of wipebreech. In any case, according to the values of the 21st-century *New York Times* at least, Thoreau had one significant advantage over No Impact Man Colin Beavan: he wasn't married.

Remarking on the part played in Beavan's project by his wife, Michelle Conlin, the *Times* observed: 'Giving up toilet paper seems a fairly profound gesture of commitment.'

'Perhaps the real guinea pig in this experiment,' the paper's reporter added, 'is the Conlin-Beavan marriage.'

At the time of writing, Beavan and Conlin remain married. Some things, it seems, are stronger even than toilet paper.

Perhaps we might wish that we could explain all this to Joseph C Gayetty, back in 1857 – or, rather, in 1856, before he launched the Medicated Paper that changed the world. We might show him the damage being done to precious ancient forests by rapacious loo-roll tycoons. We might bewail the march of over-cossetted consumerism. We might explain to him that, all around the world, billions of people make do perfectly well without any kind of toilet paper at all, and have done so for thousands of years. We could ask him, in short, *what is the point of toilet paper?*

At around the same time as Gayetty was refining his new invention, Michael Faraday – a man of perhaps even greater genius – was being asked a similar question. WE Gladstone, the Prime Minister, wanted to know what on earth was the *use* of electricity.

Gayetty might just as well have given us the same answer as Faraday gave Gladstone.

'Why, sir,' Faraday replied, 'there is every possibility that you will soon be able to tax it!'

In 1990, New Jersey governor Jim Florio did his best. His extended sales tax, designed to tackle a $3bn deficit, brought a multitude of previously untaxed items into the taxable category. Inevitably, it became known not as the Detergents Tax or the Telecoms Tax or the Janitorial Services Tax (all of which joined TP in attracting tax) but as the Toilet Paper Tax.

Florio had hoped that, in time, New Jerseyians would come to see the tax programme as a brave and necessary measure aimed at keeping their state solvent. He seems to have been unaware that many Americans love their toilet paper almost as much as they hate paying their taxes. New Jersey became a focal-point for anti-taxation protestors. A local radio station stopped playing music and started broadcasting anti-Toilet Paper Tax propaganda. In the Senate, Republican Senator Lee B Laskin argued against the tax by bringing a stack of loo-rolls into the debating chamber with him and brandishing them angrily to drive home his points.

The real or imagined prospect of a Toilet Paper Tax has been used ever since as a stick with which to beat US politicians.

If this is what happens when you simply try and add a few cents or pence to the cost of a roll, the upshot if anyone tried to ban the stuff outright is terrible to think of. A global uprising would surely result, perhaps rallying behind a battle-cry to echo that of pro-gun campaigner Charlton Heston: *'I'll give you my bumfodder when you pry it from my cold, dead hands.'*

Conclusion

Things could have been worse. If not for us, then certainly for the geese.

Suggested further reading

Aristophanes, *The Complete Plays*, Paul Roche trans. (New American Library, 2005)
The kind of toilet humour that echoes down the ages.

Baker, Nicholson, *The Mezzanine* (Granta, 2011)
If you're interested in toilet paper, you may well be interested in drinking straws, shoelaces and how to apply deodorant when you've already tucked your shirt in. In which case, this is the novel for you.

Bourke, J.G., *The Portable Scatalog: Excerpts from Scatalogic Rites of All Nations*, L. Kaplan ed. (William Morrow & Co, 1994)
Snippets from Bourke's legendarily eye-opening (if scholastically unsound) atlas of human toilet practices. Covers everything bar bumfodder.

Friedman, SGM Herbert A., *Strange Gifts From Above* (www.psywarrior.com/GiftsFromAbove.html)
Staggering examples from the history of bumfodder-themed psyops.

Hart-Davis, Adam, *Thunder, Flush And Thomas Crapper* (Michael O'Mara Books, 1997)
A thoroughgoing toilet A to Z, with, as you might expect, a focus on the nuts and bolts of boghouse-building and crapper design.

Hennig, Jean-Luc, *The Rear View: A Brief And Elegant History Of Bottoms Through The Ages*, M. Crosland and E. Powell trans. (Souvenir Press, 1995)

A poetic and learned odyssey through pre- and post-modern notions of the bum.

Horan, Julie, *Sitting Pretty: An Uninhibited History Of The Toilet* (Robson Books, 1998)
A treasure-trove of lavatorial anecdote.

Muir, Frank, *An Irreverent And Almost Complete History Of The Bathroom* (Heinemann, 1982)
A jolly and unembarrassed stroll through the privy-places of the past.

Praeger, Dave, *Poop Culture* (Feral House, 2007)
This book will change the way you think about going to the toilet. If you don't think about going to the toilet, this book will see to it that you do.

Rabelais, Francois, *Gargantua And Pantagruel* (Penguin Classics, 2006)
The Alpha and Omega of experimental *torcheculism*. Gargantua teaches us that no taboo is too precious to challenge, no idea is too disgusting to wring a laugh out of, and – most importantly – nothing is too strange to try wiping your bottom on.

Rickards, Maurice and Twynman, Michael, *The Encyclopedia of Ephemera: A Guide to the Fragmentary Documents of Everyday Life for the Collector, Curator, and Historian* (Routledge, 2000)
On the importance of the things we throw away. A valuable treasury of bumf.

Sale, Charles, *The Specialist* (Souvenir Press, 1994)
Gentle wit from the golden age of outhouse, corncob and dry-goods catalogue.

ROLL OF HONOUR

The pioneers who shaped the wiping world

Joseph C. Gayetty
The medicated paper man. He liked it so much, he put his name on it (but not, alas, his 'bland smile' © *New Orleans Medical News and Hospital Gazette*).

Emperor Hongwu
No, he didn't invent the stuff. Yes, he was a brutal, tyrannical bastard. But he *did* place what is believed to be the first bulk order for toilet-paper, and therefore deserves to be remembered, if only as the spiritual father of the facilities-management sector.

François Rabelais
Without Rabelais, it would probably never have even *occurred* to anyone that a goose's neck – never mind a Spanish hat, a lawyer's briefcase or a stray cat – could be used to swab one's bumgut, perinee or nockhole. *Chapeau, monsieur.*

Jonathan Swift
Seldom can a man in Holy Orders have so unblushingly revelled in the basest forms of toilet humour. If the Archbishop of Canterbury were only half as forthright, perhaps the modern church wouldn't be in the state it is today.

Aristophanes
Many of the Athenian's satirical asides are about as funny to a modern audience as a Shakespeare pun or a *Carry On* film. But his favourite theme – basically, the application of damp *spongion* to soiled *proctos* – never grows old.